D1286962

TWAYNE'S
RULERS AND STATESMEN OF THE WORLD
SERIES

Hans L. Trefousse, Brooklyn College
General Editor

BERNARDO O'HIGGINS

(*TROW 8*)

Bernardo O'Higgins

By JAY KINSBRUNER

Queens College
of the City University of New York

Twayne Publishers, Inc. :: New York

Library of Congress Catalog Card Number: 67–28863

MANUFACTURED IN THE UNITED STATES OF AMERICA

For Mickey and Susan

Introduction

I undertook this short examination of Bernardo O'Higgins and his era basically for two reasons. First, the English-speaking world has no recent, or even reasonably recent, study of the man and the age. The last one published in English to my knowledge is John J. Mehegan's *O'Higgins of Chile,* a pleasantly written account that appeared in London in 1913. Second, I was not at all satisfied with the existing interpretations of either O'Higgins or the period. It seemed an encouraging situation: a publisher wanting a book and a historian who specializes in nineteenth-century Chile desiring to make known his views. Emphasis in this volume is placed on interpretation. The basic facts can be found in many places, perhaps most obviously in Jaime Eyzaguirre's *Bernardo O'Higgins,* published in Chile in Spanish. I do not hesitate to point this out since I also examined the documents relative to O'Higgins' life: his letters, the newspapers published during his career, letters of his colleagues, his decrees, and the congressional records. And at any rate, Eyzaguirre's popular study is best appreciated for its qualities as a synthesis of known facts rather than a source of new information. However, I would hardly have attempted a new biography of Don Bernardo for a Chilean audience since I could have made my opinions known to it in the form of articles. Readers familiar with Chilean historiography might come away with the impression that I relied to a great extent on Francisco A. Encina's massive twenty-volume *Historia De Chile.* Actually, both Encina and I focused our pedestrian attention upon Diego Barros Arana's *Historia Jeneral De Chile,* the masterful multi-volume work by one of Chile's leading nineteenth-century historians with which all subsequent scholars have had to reckon . . . one way or another.

Since my central concern is interpretation, I should like to clarify several underlying themes at the outset. Characterization of one's views in an introductory note is very much a precarious business with the end result often an oversimplification. But in order to enable the general reader to achieve a more meaningful insight into the period, I shall attempt to do so.

It is almost as if the two major events of the story related in this book should not have occurred at all: that Chile should not have struck out for independence, and that Bernardo O'Higgins should not have become Supreme Director. Nothing in the prior history of either—of Chile or O'Higgins—could allow one to suspect the eventuality of these developments. That they came to pass is rather more a measure of the uniqueness of the era than of special qualities inherent in the country or the man. Events in the Iberian Peninsula—the Napoleonic invasion of 1807-1808—induced the Chileans, as well as many other Americans, to take the first steps toward independence. Long-standing grievances against the colonial system, especially the rather urgent need for a political economy attentive to the needs of Chile's immediate situation, contrived to make palatable, and in some cases even popular, the virtual independence that Chile enjoyed after the establishment of the Junta of 1810 in the name of the deposed King Ferdinand VII. While I do not subscribe to a Marxist interpretation of the role of economics in the independence movement, I do recognize that economics directly encouraged many Chileans toward complete independence after 1810. However, in Chile as elsewhere, some Creoles—Americans of Spanish descent—no doubt chanced to suffer economically by a thorough break with the mother country.

Nor do I subscribe to the thesis that by 1813 a desire on the part of a significant number of Creoles to replace the *peninsulares* —those born in Spain—in the governmental bureaucracy contributed to the final contrivance of independence. The fact is that the main body of the bureaucracy was not altered with independence. Creoles constituted the actual working bureaucracy both before and after independence. However, not all were patriots. Creoles even sat in the major lay and religious tribunals. By the close of the colonial period they were overtly restricted only from the office of Intendant. Perhaps it is natural to assume that Creoles coveted this position—and an easier accessibility to other positions as well—avidly enough to fight for independence after the invasion from Peru in 1813. But I have found no documentation to indicate the validity of such an assumption. In an attempt to summarize the independence movement for a book about Chilean history in the post-1829 era, I observed that Chile did not possess quite enough qualified personnel to indulge her self-imposed republicanism.[1] As a consequence of the research carried out for the present book, I not longer find this statement personally attractive. The Chilean government after 1810 did not lack qualified personnel.[2] For the cause of governmental instability after 1817, and especially the disruptive near-anarchical period between 1823 and 1829, one must search further than this.

When speaking of qualified personnel I am not referring to O'Higgins or his successor General Ramón Freire. These men, in fact, were in many ways unsuited to their positions. Both were supported by competent ministers, congressmen, judges, militarists, and provincial officials; but they themselves left much to be desired as Supreme Directors. O'Higgins was the Chilean military hero of the independence movement, a movement carried to fruition by an army whose sponsor was Buenos Aires, whose origin was the province of Cuyo, and whose leader was General José de San Martín. The independence of Chile after the 1814 expulsion of the patriot army was but one aspect of an Argentine plan for the liberation of the entire South American continent. Not only did Chile owe its freedom to the United Provinces of Río de la Plata (which later became Argentina and for which the term Argentine will be used where convenient in this book), but also the very nature of its new government in 1817. This is clear in the relationship of San Martín and the *Logia lautarina* to O'Higgins. Yet the most impressive manifestation of this is the person of O'Higgins himself. He represented the Argentine grand scheme of independence in Chile, both to the Argentines and the Chileans. In a very real sense Chilean independence resulted from a zealous patriotic momentum that started in Buenos Aires, crossed the Andes into Chile, and then sailed north to Peru where it faltered through its own inertia. That momentum in Chile, which permitted a war-ravaged country to mount a major military offensive after 1817, was potent and efficacious enough to assuage the virulence of innumerable ills. But by 1823 the situation had altered considerably. Now the momentum was gone; it was time for Chilean nationalism to assert itself. Certainly O'Higgins was a Chilean and a nationalist, but he represented something both more and less—depending on one's point of view—than nationalism after independence was established firmly.

More than any other single factor, O'Higgins' fall from power in 1823 reflects this new national sentiment. The existence of this dualism—the presence of a Chilean national government of foreign origin founded upon a patriotic base that continuously developed a fervent national aspiration—is a basic theme of the present book.[3] The governments after 1823 were thoroughly national in both origin and direction. That they failed to achieve stability was not due to the lack of qualified personnel; in fact, the success of the governments after 1829 was due in no small part to a very clear presence of qualified personnel.

One other theme pervades this book. Because of the careless manner in which it has been used, the term "landed aristocracy" has become a relatively meaningless epithet. Several writers have noted the existence of a rather large and powerful capitalist class of merchants and miners in Chile by the 1850's. I have attempted to demonstrate that this was the case already by 1829.[4] Although the topic requires further study, I have come to the conclusion at this time that even by 1817 the landed aristocracy did not govern Chile exclusively. Men of landed wealth were either patriots or royalists according to no recognizable pattern. Between 1810 and 1829 the primary source of wealth in Chile was land and commerce in agricultural products. The great majority of landowners were not aristocrats. In 1810 Chile had a population of less than 1,000,000, including about 100,000 Araucanian Indians. Most of the white inhabitants lived between La Serena to the north and the Bío-Bío River to the south. The province of Santiago held about 500,000 people, the province of Coquimbo (Coquimbo became a province in 1811) about 75,000, and the province of Concepción about 200,000. Since most of the agricultural and commercial wealth centered in Santiago, as well as the population, one might assume that the landed aristocrats of that province generally governed Chile. This was hardly the case. True, many of the leading government officials were from families that possessed land, but this was a commonplace in a country such as Chile where land was plentiful and the price was not prohibitive. And not all sons of the landed rich worked on the land. Many were military, civil, or religious employees by career. No one has yet demonstrated that their beliefs ran contrary to the times or were inconsonant with those of the merchants, miners, moneylenders, sailors, and so on, except insofar as they may have desired to preserve the *mayorazgo*—the entailed estate.

This is not to say that the society was democratic. At times to vote or hold office one had to possess real property or liquid capital. It is sad to note that farmhands, domestic employees, and people in debt to the public treasury were eliminated, although not permanently, from the active citizenry. But this citizenry was notably pluralistic, and its government was highly representative of the enfranchised Chilean population at large. The term "landed aristocracy" does not indicate the true nature of that part of the Chilean population which governed Chile between 1810 and the end of O'Higgins' tenure in 1823.

Acknowledgments

Once again I am pleased to acknowledge my great debt to the staffs of the Biblioteca Nacional De Chile and the Archivo Nacional De Chile, and the New York Public Library, for the many courtesies extended over the past few years. I should like to thank Professor John E. Fagg of New York University and Professor Magnus Mörner of Queens College for reading and criticizing the entire manuscript. Since I followed my own instincts on certain points and matters of approach, the mistakes that appear certainly are the fault of the author. Lastly, I should like to thank Mr. and Mrs. Raymond Parker of Kiamesha Lake, New York, for their kind hospitality during a time when much of this book was written, and Mr. George Parker for his technical assistance in the preparation of the map.

Contents

Chronology

1763	Ambrosio Higgins arrives in Chile.
1778	Bernardo O'Higgins born in Chillán.
1783	Bernardo is baptized.
1790	Bernardo Riquelme (O'Higgins) to Lima.
1794	Bernardo to Spain and then England.
1799	Back to Spain.
1800	Contracts yellow fever.
1802	To Chile.
1808	Ferdinand VII deposed.
1810	First national Junta created in Santiago.
1811	First national Congress convened in Santiago.
1813	First invasion from Peru.
1814	Battle of Rancagua.
1814–1817	The reconquest of Chile.
1817	Bernardo O'Higgins becomes Supreme Director of Chile.
1818	Battle of Maipo.
1818	Provisional Constitution promulgated.
1820	*Expedición Libertadora* departs for Peru.
1822	Permanent Constitution adopted.
1823	Bernardo O'Higgins resigns and goes into exile in Peru.
1842	Bernardo O'Higgins dies in Peru.

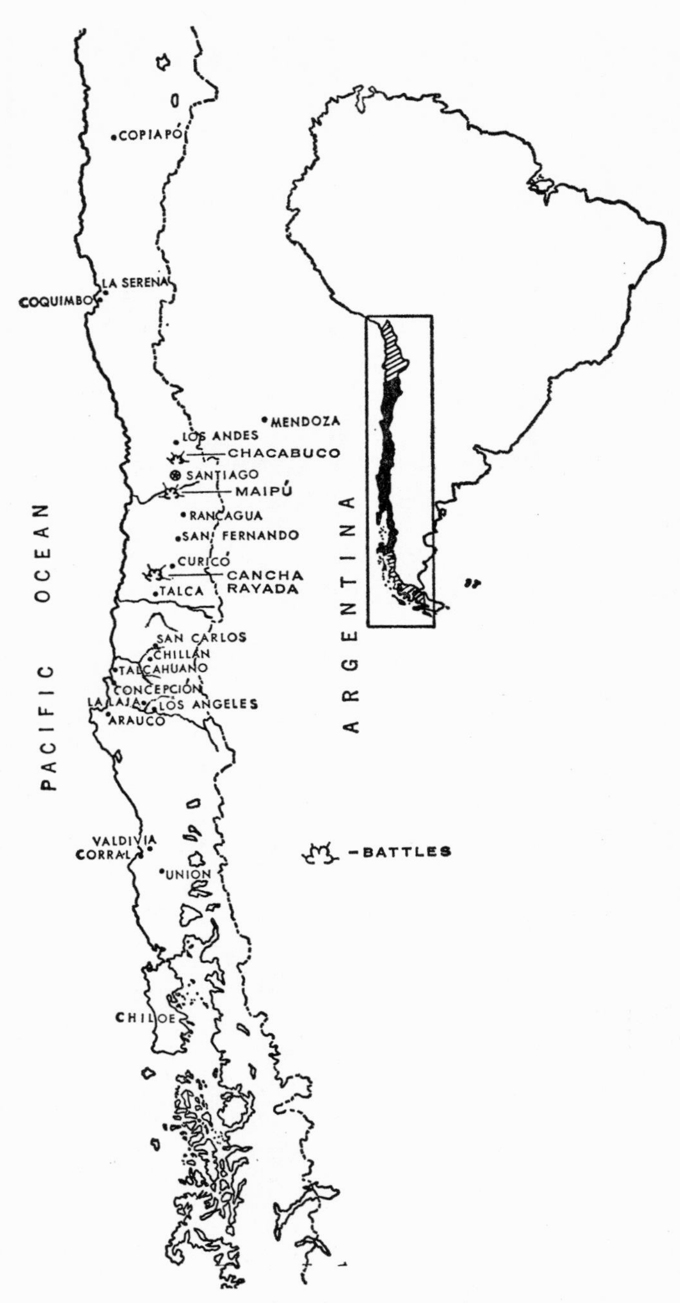

Chile during the independence movement.

CHAPTER I

His Youth

BERNARDO O'HIGGINS WAS PROBABLY BORN ON AUGUST 20, 1778, IN the town of Chillán and baptized five years later at Talca. Actually it was his second baptism but the first in which his name appeared in the official record. This was not an unusual circumstance for a child born out of wedlock. As noted in the certificate of baptism, Bernardo O'Higgins was the son of Ambrosio O'Higgins, Colonel of His Majesty's Royal Armies, single, and a leading lady of Chillán, also single, whose name, for her reputation, was withheld from the document.

In the entire history of colonial Latin America few names are more unusual than Ambrosio O'Higgins, or as he referred to himself, Higgins. Born in Ireland somewhere around the year 1720, he had gone to Spain as a youth to visit a kinsman, under whose protection he received an education. In the early 1750's he worked for Irish merchants in Cádiz. He arrived in Buenos Aires in 1757 and then proceeded to Chile, but his commercial ventures probably were not successful since in 1759 he returned to Spain. By the end of 1763 he was back in Chile and this time working for the Chilean government in the construction of fortifications. It is not known whether he had ever received formal training as an engineer, but it is certain that he was highly competent as an administrator. In 1778 Chile became a Captaincy-General, that is, something more than a province and less than a viceroyalty. Such a designation was reserved by the Crown for frontier regions where a relatively effective and distinctly military government was required. Chile's military problem was the Araucanian Indian to the south of Concepción. Although probably the most successful of the fighting Indian populations in Latin America, the Araucanians were some distance from Santiago, where the Captain-General resided. Perhaps as a consequence of that distance and in recognition of the Captain-General's traditional role as President of the Audiencia—the supreme court—decidedly a more civilian employ, the Chileans continued to refer to their governor as President.

But Chile was still a frontier colony, and when not actually at war the President's chief concern was usually the construction and maintenance of fortifications in the south. This was no place for a civilian, and Ambrosio Higgins was incorporated into the Royal Army. Soon he was a colonel and Intendant of Concepción, the highest local official. In 1788 he became President of Chile. Higgins was one of the best governors in Chilean history. Much to the delight of the active Chilean population, as well as the Crown, he concentrated on internal improvements. New roads were constructed, most notably one to connect Santiago with the port of Valparaíso. New cities were founded; fortifications were modernized. In 1796 he was granted the title of Marquis of Vallenar and Osorno and designated Viceroy of Peru. From this position he did not forget the needs of Chile.

That a displaced Irishman should become a Spanish noble and governor of a leading viceroyalty in America is strong indication that the Spanish colonial system was considerably less static and closed than one might think. This was the era of the Enlightenment in Europe and of the Bourbon reforms in Spain and America. From the middle of the eighteenth century, the Crown (now Bourbon rather than Hapsburg) began initiating a reform in the colonial system to provide for better prospects of defense, to raise revenues, to insure the territorial integrity of the empire against the intrusion of foreign nations, and to lessen the chance of popular rebellion. Thus, a fresh approach was adopted in both political and economic administration. Liberal trade decrees were promulgated; Creoles now became part of the military officialdom for the first time; new scientific methods were introduced; scientific and literary societies were patronized by Spanish ministers of state; new techniques of administration, from the intendancy system all the way down to improved methods of bookkeeping, were adopted; and, perhaps most symptomatic of the enlightened attitude, the Jesuits were expelled. It was a transitional stage, often erratic in approach and application, sometimes a success, at other times inflicting rather disastrous results. In some places the traditional social, political, and economic stagnation continued to persevere; in others a vibrant atmosphere conjoined with the Creole wealth—both new and old—to inspire renewed faith in the colonial system, or, depending on how one was affected by the reforms, a desire for further innovation.

It was during his tenure as Intendant of Concepción that middle-aged Ambrosio Higgins had an affair with the very youthful Isabel Riquelme. With funds provided by the Intendant, the

Riquelme family, socially comfortable but of modest economic means, established mother and son in a home in Chillán. Bernardo Riquelme was recognized and accepted by his mother's large family. But he did not remain for long at his birthplace. In 1782 a lieutenant of dragoons under orders from the Intendant arrived in Chillán, collected the child and, without indicating his destination, proceeded to Talca.

While Ambrosio Higgins conducted no official business with the family and had no direct personal contact with his child, it is quite apparent that he was determined to influence Bernardo's development. The child was placed in the home of one of Higgins' most intimate friends, Juan Albano Pereira. Portuguese by birth, a merchant by profession, Albano chose the Plate River estuary as his home in America, but he was captured by the Spaniards when they took Colonia del Sacramento from the Portuguese in 1762 and interned at Mendoza. It was there that he was granted permission to establish himself in Chile proper. (Mendoza was then a part of Chile.) Albano became a prosperous merchant in Talca and made an excellent marriage. Bernardo was welcomed into the Albano household as both son and brother. Casimiro Albano, born in 1783, was to become an influential patriot, priest, Senator, diplomat, and loyal supporter of his "brother" Bernardo.

The father often received reports concerning his son's progress. In 1787 Juan Martínez de Rozas, later a principal leader of the early independence period, was appointed counselor (*asesor*) to the Intendant of Concepción. During his trip from Santiago to Concepción he stayed three days in the Albano household. There he met Bernardo. Juan Albano made it clear to Rozas that the youth was the Intendant's natural son. Afraid that neither he nor Ambrosio would live a good deal longer, the old gentleman considered it wise to impart this confidence to a trusted government official. Rozas accepted the charge of secrecy and assured Albano that he would testify to the boy's parentage should that be necessary in the future. Once in Concepción Rozas became both a colleague and friend of the Intendant, even living in his house. Many times, Rozas later recalled, the Intendant spoke of the child Bernardo. He often told Rozas that he wanted to send the boy to Spain for his education.

Bernardo probably saw his father for the first time in 1788 when the newly appointed President of Chile stayed a short while with the Albanos on his way to Santiago. Even under such circumstances we can only assume that the two met or that the boy still known as Bernardo Riquelme, was aware of the relationship at that date. The father must have decided that it was time for his son to commence some sort of formal education. For this purpose a Franciscan monastery in Chillán was selected. The boy was sent back to his birthplace. Since the expulsion of the Jesuits in 1767 the Franciscans of Chillán spent most of their time and energy in the supervision of the neighboring Indian communities. Yet they continued to enjoy a considerable reputation for teaching and scholarship.

Though as Ambrosio well understood the facilities at the disposal of the Franciscans were limited. In 1790 he decided to send the boy to Lima. But by now twelve-year-old Bernardo Riquelme was very much a part of his maternal family, who were not eager for a second separation. Thus, an official acting for the father had to make secret arrangements with the Franciscans to send the boy north. Bernardo's relationship with the friars, especially his immediate tutor Fra Gil Calvo, was warm and friendly. It would later be vexatious, when during the independence struggle the Franciscans would remain loyal to the Crown.[1]

Lima was the viceregal capital, aristocratic, stable, and incontinently proud of her prominent position in Spain's American system. Bernardo spent four years in the *colegio*—high school—of San Carlos pursuing studies mainly in Latin and philosophy. His boyhood friends at the school were later to play significant parts in the Peruvian independence movement, making Peru a likely place of exile for Bernardo in the not too distant future. In 1794 Bernardo Riquelme was sixteen years old and about to enter a critical phase of his development: The next years would be the least satisfying of his life. Ambrosio made arrangements for his son to study in Europe.

Thus in mid-1794 the youth embarked at Callao for Cádiz. There he was placed under the protection of a very prosperous Chilean merchant, Nicolás de la Cruz, one of his father's friends. Cruz was born in Talca and was now related through marriage to Juan Albano Pereira. Though not especially well educated himself, he avidly collected books and sponsored scholarship. For some unexplained reason the relationship between Cruz and Bernardo was always on the frigid side. Cruz was Bernardo's immediate protector in Europe, and it was left up to him to make arrangements necessary for the youth to proceed to England for his education. It is not clear why Ambrosio now favored England rather than Spain.

Bernardo was seventeen when he entered the English-speaking

world, the bastard son of an Irish President of Chile. Considering his later career, the English period was perhaps the most influential in his progress toward maturity. Not only were his views changed, but he discovered a different way of life, which continued to be a point of reference throughout his manhood. But this is not to say that it was the happiest season of his life. His English guardians, two London watchmakers named Spencer and Perkins, placed him in a small boarding school in nearby Richmond. There he studied and mastered the English language. He spoke and wrote it with great facility. French proved a little less successful; he could read it well but had trouble with pronunciation. There were other courses, such as history, geography, painting, and music. From this experience dates his lifelong interest in the piano.

It was a time also of ideas. Bernardo cultivated a sense of national pride for Chile while in foreign residence. He seems to have spent considerable time with Ercilla's *La Araucana* and Molina's *Historia de Chile*. But more important, there were men bold in action and thought who appeared anxious for his companionship. Most significant was the Venezuelan precursor of Latin American independence, Francisco Miranda. This frenetic patriot could claim participation in the American Revolution and the French Revolution. In London he created a lodge, which later became known as *Lautarina*. No doubt it influenced the subsequent establishment of the *Logia lautarina* in Buenos Aires by Alvear and San Martín in 1812, and the Chilean branch founded in 1817. Several American patriots joined the London lodge, including Bernardo Riquelme. Through membership they were dedicated to the independence of Latin America. It was a rather remarkable position for the son of the Viceroy of Peru to take. Before he left England in 1799, Bernardo received a letter from his preceptor that reflects the student-teacher relationship between the two as well as the intellectual conception that drew them together. Miranda enjoined the youth to remember always that only in England and the United States could one opine freely about politics. He was told to love his Chile, never forget the state of subjugation in which it lived, and work every day for its salvation. Interestingly, Miranda observed that not every king or clergyman was an enemy of the rights of man. "I know through experience that in this class exist the most enlightened and liberal men in South America, but the difficulty is in finding them." Always aware of the value of theatrics, Miranda closed by ordering his political student to read the letter every day of his trip to

Spain and then destroy it. "Do not forget neither the Inquisition, nor its spies, nor its dungeons, nor its tortures." [2] Surely Bernardo, twenty-one, was impressed.

Whether or not the young man desired to remain in England is not clear. His constant state of penury probably induced him to travel to Spain. Ambrosio had made provisions for Cruz to receive fifteen hundred pesos annually to provide for the boy. This was certainly satisfactory, but somehow en route from Cruz to his Spanish intermediary in England, Romero, to Spencer and Perkins, and then on to the boarding school and tutors, the amount dwindled to the point of being insufficient. Someone along the line was dealing in less than good faith. It was not difficult to exaggerate expenses. To Cruz the son of the Marquis of Vallenar and Osorno lamented his exigent state. Perkins no longer cared to be burdened by a responsibility that carried so little financial advantage. Bernardo estimated that he required only six additional months to perfect his education, but presently he was without a tutor. He asked for advice. But Cruz chose to be silent, and the situation did not improve. Several London merchants, hearing of the young man's plight and distance from home, joined together to lend him about ten pesos each month. He wrote to Cruz again a year later, in 1799, that his "situation is such that instead of learning and progressing in the various things to which I have applied myself, I am beginning to forget them through a lack of instruction. . . ." He solicited permission to travel directly to America, "since I have some merchant friends who promise to give me free passage from here to the island of Trinidad or Philadelphia, and from there I can proceed to seek my life in Spanish America, where, however bad things be never can they be worse than here."

Through all this Bernardo continually courted his father's affection. He wrote to the Viceroy several times but never received an answer. The first letter we have is dated 1799. Bernardo commenced by referring to Ambrosio as "Beloved father of my soul and my greatest well-wisher. . . ." For such liberty he begged forgiveness, although it was not clear to him whether he should or should not use such an intimate expression. He was only following what nature ("until now my only teacher") had taught. He was going to evoke a paternal response from the old man: "and if you would have different instructions, I would obey them." At this he failed. He did not speak of his poverty, and in fact noted that he knew that his father had provided "all the requirements for my education." Just when Bernardo knew that

Higgins was his father and that he was paying for his education is not certain. Bernardo considered himself at least twenty-one years old—he was probably a little younger—and without a career or the prospects of one. If it could be arranged, he hoped to enter a military academy specializing in navigation. He felt an inclination for such a career, and he observed to the Viceroy that the military life had advantages. Meanwhile, "I only await with anxiety the orders of Your Excellency in order to obey and undertake that which Your Excellency commands. . . ." Perhaps there would be a command.

Rather than sailing directly for America as he had proposed, Bernardo traveled to Cádiz in the spring of 1799. According to his travel papers, which historian Benjamín Vicuña Mackenna had in his possession when he wrote *El ostracismo del jeneral d. Bernardo O'Higgins,* Bernardo was five feet and six inches tall, broad of shoulder, and somewhat heavier than his height should have allowed esthetically. Thick black hair, blue eyes, and a short nose made the young man rather easy to look at.[3] Owing to the hostilities between England and Spain, Bernardo could sail only as far as Lisbon. From there he proceeded to Cádiz, where he once again stayed with the Cruz family. It appears that he wanted to join the Spanish army, but was dissuaded by Cruz, who suggested that to be an officer one had to produce a birth certificate and that the irregularities of his circumstance might cause an embarrassment.[4] One cannot be sure why he chose the Spanish army.

Bernardo's stay in Spain promised to be no more pleasant than the English interval. He resided in an inhospitable household without employment or an independent source of income. The provocative question of Spanish American independence continued to absorb his attention. It was here that he came into contact with two clerics who favored independence. One was Juan Pablo Fretes, Argentine by birth, but later Canon of the Cathedral of Santiago and a president of Chile's first national Congress. And as always his irksome familial problems added to his loneliness. How great his sadness, he wrote in February 1800, for not having received a single letter from his mother. He pleaded with her for "that motherly love due a son." She should write him in care of a friend in Buenos Aires. Obviously he planned to depart for America.

And he did, but it was an unsuccessful voyage. After booking passage on the merchant frigate "Confianza" he waited more than three months for its departure to Buenos Aires. A convoy of twelve merchant ships with an escort of four royal warships sailed on April 3. The first four days were uneventful, but at three in the morning on April 7 the convoy sighted the sails of three large English warships. Several ships escaped, but the "Confianza" was captured and taken to Gibraltar. Bernardo passed himself off as an Englishman and served as interpreter. But this earned him slight consideration. They "robbed me of everything I had, although little, leaving me only with what I had on," he informed his father from Cádiz later in April. He was without food for three days. From Gibraltar he made his way to Algeciras, "half enfeebled from hunger, heat and fatigue. . . ." There he "had the good fortune of meeting Captain don Tomás O'Higgins, who also was made a prisoner on the frigate *Florentina,* where he was a passenger." Also short of funds, O'Higgins gave Bernardo—his cousin and soon to be his military colleague in the fight for Chilean independence—a peso. Bernardo booked passage on board a ship headed for Cádiz, "offering to pay it upon my arrival. . . . The day after our departure we were again pursued by the English."

A sad, bewildered young man reached Cádiz only to find it unavoidable to impose on the reluctant hospitality of Nicolás de la Cruz. To his father he wrote: "I have abandoned all hopes of seeing my father, mother and my country. . . ." And the closing: "Goodbye, beloved father, until the heavens grant me the pleasure of embracing you; until then I will not be content, nor happy. I send Your Excellency the heart of a son who so much esteems and desires to see you." The Viceroy probably inferred that his son was planning to return immediately to America, and since it would take several months for the trip, or perhaps a year, it seems that the old man stopped sending funds to Cruz. At the end of June he again wrote to his father: "I am also pained by the sight of myself incarcerated in this sad Europe without being able to find even one remedy or friend who can help or liberate me from her." Since his unscheduled return to Spain, he had had no money to spend, but he had not been a nuisance to anyone in this matter. Though this had caused him to suffer "all the inconveniences imaginable even to the point of depriving myself of the privilege of leaving my room due to the lack of means for the decency of a man of modesty. . . ." He asked his father to send money and closed with a plea for communication. How he envied his friends the letters they received from home. "But me, poor luckless one! From no one."

Things got worse. Bernardo's only possession of value was a piano he had left at Cádiz when he first started out for America. Now he sold it to raise enough money to travel to Lisbon, where he hoped to find a ship destined for Rio de Janeiro. But sickness interrupted his plans. A plague of yellow fever struck Cádiz in the middle of August 1800, and in a matter of two months took over thirty-seven hundred lives. Altogether, more than forty-seven thousand inhabitants of greater Cádiz were stricken. Bernardo was one of them. At the time, he was at the neighboring port of San Lúcar de Barrameda. To his father he wrote that he was attacked by the yellow fever "with all its fury, and on the third day of my sickness by black vomit." The last rites were administered immediately. The physicians demonstrated so little hope that Bernardo himself had to ask for a dose of the cinchona bark from which quinine is made. The physicians awaited his expiration, but after a few hours he began to progress. The black vomiting continued, but he started to feel relief.

Once again it was necessary for Bernardo to place himself in the Cruz household. In December he wrote his father that he was living there, "a man beaten and abandoned to human misery, without even a friend whom one can approach for his aid and advice. . . ." Merely "the idea that I have to continue in that house, kills me." In the space of two years he had not had one single word with Cruz, nor any financial succor. For his trip to Buenos Aires he had purchased six shirts and a pair of trousers, but all that was lost to the English. The money from the sale of the piano went in part to pay his medical bills. The hundred remaining pesos were given to Cruz to settle old accounts. His formal education had come to a complete halt.

All at once news from home began to reach him. From his mother he received a less than inspiring letter, his first, in which she mentioned mostly domestic problems and the loss of her father. A Franciscan from Chillán on his way through Spain informed Bernardo that an element at court was preparing his father's downfall. And then the ultimate humiliation of his Spanish sojourn: a letter from the Viceroy to Cruz. Bernardo was informed by Cruz that his father's health continued to be good, but that the old gentleman was disturbed by his son's conduct. Since his son had proved himself incapable of pursuing any career and was ungrateful for the favors granted him, the Viceroy ordered that he leave the Cruz household. To his father Bernardo wrote a lengthy and passionate defense of himself in early January 1801. "I, sir, do not know what offense I have committed for such punishment, nor do I know in what way I have been ungrateful (an offense I abhor most), since throughout my life I have endeavored with all earnestness to give pleasure to Your Excellency, and upon seeing this my only pretension frustrated, irritating my father and protector, I have become confused." In this Bernardo was probably sincere. Throughout his life he would demonstrate an inability to perceive the possible implications of his actions. In this case, his activities in England might well have impugned the Viceroy's reputation. His father died on March 18, 1801, and consequently never received the letter. But Bernardo wrote again, early in March. He had probably reached the most forlorn, pessimistic stage of his life. "It seems that misfortune has destined me to live in an unknown corner, full of necessities and all imaginable miseries without finding out where or how to start a career, unknown to all the world, without determination and no art for flattery, one of the leading sciences. . . ."

Perhaps it was this arid period, so exasperatingly void of familial love, that evoked Bernardo's later paternal and even overprotective attitude toward the Chilean population. In his maturity he would prefer private to public life, but would hardly be an ascetic. Rather, he seems to have enjoyed the excitation and panoply of high office. Yet he would expect Chileans to conform to his rigid interpretation of what was good for them, even in banal social matters.

News of the Viceroy's passing considerably altered his situation. The announcement mentioned an inheritance for him, and he rapidly made plans to cross the Atlantic to collect whatever his father willed him as well perhaps as his cherished birthright—his father's name. Now he had no difficulty financing a trip, being at last a good business risk. However, the English fleet was still blockading the Spanish coast and, since the recent Spanish declaration of war against Portugal, the rest of the Iberian Peninsula also. But with the Peace of Amiens celebrated with England in late March 1802, plans were made to ship merchant goods to Chile directly for the first time in five years. On April 14, 1802, Bernardo sailed from Cádiz on the frigate "Aurora," destined for Chile. One hundred and forty-six days later the "Aurora," after a comparatively even, placid voyage, dropped anchor at Valparaíso and announced the resumption of direct commerce with Spain.

CHAPTER II

Early Maturity in Chile

ONCE HE ARRIVED IN CHILE BERNARDO HAD TO DECIDE WHETHER HE should remain or proceed on to Lima where he might better look into the legal questions of his inheritance. In Santiago at the time was his friend and first cousin, Tomás O'Higgins, whom he sought out for advice. O'Higgins had served his uncle in Peru and had some familiarity with colonial bureaucratic procedures. Bernardo became a welcome guest in his cousin's Santiago house.

For the first time he saw a copy of the will. The executors were José de Gorbea y Vadillo, criminal prosecutor to the Audiencia of Lima, and Father Agustín Doría. The will mentioned as his bequest a large hacienda called Canteras on the island of La Laja* in southern Chile, with three thousand head of cattle. Since the late Viceroy, as well as every colonial official upon completion of his term, was even in death subjected to a *residencia*—an investigation of one's administration of office that sometimes lasted several years—the executors maintained control over the estate so that claims against the Viceroy or his estate might be satisfied if the *juez de residencia* so decreed.

For some reason it took Bernardo, now referring to himself as Bernardo O'Higgins de Riquelme, until September to communicate directly with the executors in Lima. He wrote them indicating his impoverished state, and that the only recourse left him in order to survive was to take possession of the hacienda called Canteras. He suggested that Canteras was not subject to the *residencia* since his father obtained it before becoming Viceroy. But even if the hacienda were considered subject to the *residencia* it would be better for everyone concerned if he took control. After all, it was in his interest to raise the value of the land and cattle. It was strangely ingenuous reasoning for a twenty-four-year-old man of the world to formulate. The administrator of the hacienda, Pedro Nolasco del Río, should be ordered to turn over the hacienda to Bernardo for two reasons: one, he needed it; two, the

* Though it enjoyed the name, La Laja was not an island. See map.

value would not decrease since it was in his best interest not to let that happen.

While awaiting a reply Bernardo went south to Chillán for a visit with his family. His return after an absence of twelve years was celebrated enthusiastically. Isabel Riquelme had married Angel Rodríguez of Chillán, but was soon widowed. Their one child, Rosa, would play a prominent role in her half-brother's later public career. It was probably here that Bernardo received an answer from the executors. He was informed that claims had already been made against the estate. The hacienda could be given to him temporarily only if he agreed to sell no part of it, land or livestock.[1] With this information he headed farther south to the town of Los Angeles. The island of La Laja was located in the district also called Los Angeles. Colonel Nolasco del Río, commander of the local dragoons, was happy to grant Bernardo possession of Canteras, but only under the restrictions stated by the executors. Nevertheless, Bernardo sold about five hundred head of cattle at the current price of 3½ pesos per head in order to pay for his trip from Spain and to cover past and future personal expenses until the final settlement of the will.

During the southern fall of 1803 Bernardo decided to go personally to Lima in the hope of injecting a note of haste into the lethargic proceedings. Lieutenant Colonel Tomás Delfín of the frontier forces, a former aide to Ambrosio Higgins, offered to accompany him to Lima. Delfín thought his knowledge of the Viceroy's affairs might serve to expedite matters. Bernardo informed Pedro Nolasco del Río of his intentions, and the old gentleman approved heartily.[2] He even sent a letter of recommendation to the executors. The two boarded ship for Callao in the middle of May.

Bernardo's arrival in the Spanish metropolis of South America was probably more of a homecoming than he had experienced in Santiago. It is quite likely that he had never been to the Chilean capital prior to his return from Europe, while he had lived for several years in Lima. Not only did the executors of the will receive him warmly, but several of his former schoolmates now occupied positions of substantial social importance. And he had an influential relative. The Intendant of Huamanga was Demetrio O'Higgins, another of the Viceroy's nephews. He went out of his way to be of service. Many government officials who had come under the personal protection of the Viceroy now were eager to return favors to his son. Especially influential was Manuel Urriez, Count of Ruiz de Castilla, formerly Intendant of the mercury-producing region of Huancavélica and presently President of the Audiencia of Cuzco.

Though it took several months a satisfactory arrangement was made finally. Bernardo could take possession of Canteras permanently, but he could maintain only provisional control over the livestock, which was to be used if necessary to satisfy claims against the estate or to pay for the costs of processing the will. By November he was back in Los Angeles, ready to commence what was to be personally the most satisfying interlude of his life. For seven years he would live the life of a farmer, the vocation to which he would later always consider himself best suited. One might call him a gentleman farmer, save for the fact that being an agriculturist in southern Chile in 1803 and living the life of a gentleman farmer surely had mutually exclusive connotations. Apart from the primitive state of agriculture and the distance from the dubious amenities of early nineteenth-century urban life, Los Angeles was still part of the frontier. But it was a way of life that held great attraction for him, and he brought to it enviable determination and uncommon energy. He instituted an ambitious program of breeding; houses for his workers were constructed; and granaries were erected.

Almost immediately the hacienda prospered. Living with him were his mother and sister, and together they hosted their neighbors at Canteras, government and military officials, and the local clergy. Soon he maintained a house in Chillán, where he had quite some influence through his extensive maternal family. In 1806 he became a member of the Chillán *cabildo*—the town council and the locus of Creole power in Spanish America—and began making both official and unofficial appearances in the southern capital of Concepción. It was here that he came under the patronage of Juan Martínez de Rozas, now perhaps the leading public figure in the south. At the *tertulias*—the private parties held in one's home that for centuries provided the most common form of community intercourse for the upper classes—Bernardo was introduced to and accepted by society. Since the tertulia often included an intellectual discussion of sorts, it is likely that his relatively radical political sentiments became known publicly.

Not everyone appreciated these European-inspired opinions. As a consequence of the war between England and Spain in 1804, direct trade between Chile and Europe terminated once again. The demand for goods was not satisfied by trade with Lima and animated a vast network of contraband activity. Several English and United States ships were captured and brought to the southern port of Talcahuano. The Intendant of Concepción several times called Bernardo to Concepción to act as his interpreter. It was an official relationship that did not end in a cordial friendship. Rather, the Intendant developed suspicions and doubted Bernardo's patriotism. When an English invasion of Chilean territory seemed imminent in 1807, the Intendant summoned Bernardo to Concepción ostensibly to advise the government on matters of defense, but in reality he seems to have wanted him close enough to be watched personally.[3]

Apart from the ordinary problems one would confront in adjusting to both an agricultural and urban life at the same time, two things in particular troubled Bernardo: the matter of his inheritance and his legitimization. The inheritance was settled finally in 1805. Executor Gorbea stopped off in Santiago to visit with his wife's family on his way to Spain, and took the occasion to gather all necessary papers so that he might himself take them to Spain and finally settle the estate. Gorbea had decided that about half the hacienda's livestock would be sold to cover expenses of the estate, and the remainder along with the real property would go to Bernardo. Acting under orders from Gorbea, Nolasco del Río prepared an inventory of the livestock. There were well over four thousand head of cattle of all ages on Canteras, but according to Bernardo's calculations, after subtracting the half eliminated by decree and those in ill-health, he would be left with slightly over a thousand head. Bernardo refused to sign the inventory, but Gorbea wrote that his agreement would end the matter once and for all. He signed, and Gorbea took the final papers to Spain.[4]

The question of his legitimacy was considerably more nettlesome. For reasons that were at least in part pragmatic Bernardo wanted to be known as O'Higgins. Though the Viceroy named his son in the will, he did not refer to him as Bernardo O'Higgins. In 1803 Bernardo had sent a petition for legitimization from Lima to the Council of Indies. This was a common procedure, one which often induced a favorable judgment from the Council. However, it generally took years for a ruling to be handed down. In 1806 Juan Martínez de Rozas and Tomás Delfín signed statements which attested to Bernardo's legitimacy.[5] For some reason he was never granted the right to use the O'Higgins name. But sometime during the early 1800's he adopted it on his own.

• • •

Before Bernardo O'Higgins had time to settle deeply into his new way of life, Napoleonic activity in the Iberian Peninsula threatened its very foundation. In 1808 pressure from Napoleon I caused Ferdinand VII to abdicate, and Napoleon placed his brother Joseph Bonaparte on the throne of Spain. A war of reconquest commenced at once, and a patriotic council soon began governing from Seville those Spaniards who remained loyal to the deposed Ferdinand. News of these events affected Chileans variously. It was not at all clear whether patriotism indicated loyalty to Joseph or to the provisional government at Seville. To complicate matters, Chile lacked enterprising, decisive leadership. Early in 1808 the President of Chile, Luis Muñoz de Guzmán, died unexpectedly, and according to a recent royal decree in such an event the interim presidency would go to the highest ranking military official, though at least a colonel, in Chile at the time. Thus Brigadier General García Carrasco, a Spaniard stationed in Concepción and very much a beginner in public government, became President of Chile. As his private secretary and adviser he selected the highly respected Juan Martínez de Rozas. This might well have been his first and last sensible move. Rozas was one of Chile's leading lawyers and intellectually oriented government employees. He well understood that the uncertain state of affairs in Spain and the fluid situation in Chile activated many of the dormant complaints long held by the colonists toward the inequities of the colonial system. Rozas unsuccessfully attempted to encourage the new President along a path of reform. Frustrated in Santiago, he returned to a more attentive audience in Concepción and left García Carrasco without an aide who might have proved his most important ally.

By 1809 the President's maladroit administration had brought Chile to the point of open rebellion. In response to the threat, García Carrasco adopted severe methods and alienated a considerable number of moderate Chileans who had so far supported him and the Seville government. Now loyalty to Ferdinand and opposition to García Carrasco became synonymous. It became impossible to determine the precise nature of the revolutionary fervor. In the name of Ferdinand much was said inimical to the continued existence of the present Chilean government. All of which must have raised the question among patriots and moderate reformers of what type of government might follow. The first arrests among those partisans of Ferdinand were made in the evening of May 25, 1810. Officials under orders from the President arrested the *mayorazgo* José Antonio Rojas, member of the Santiago *cabildo* and, along with Juan Martínez de Rozas, probably one of the two most vociferous and influential promoters for the replacement of García Carrasco with a junta loyal to Ferdinand. The attorney for the *cabildo,* Juan Antonio de Ovalle Silva, and the Argentine lawyer, Bernardo Vera Pintado, were also arrested. On May 26 the three were sent to Valparaíso, from which port the President planned to transport them to Lima.

The patriots had their *cause célèbre.* Three very distinguished citizens were detained and ordered out of Chile without any pretense of legal procedure. The exile was opposed by their rather large and well-connected families, the *cabildo* of Santiago, by leading clergymen and businessmen, and even by the Audiencia. In the face of such sentiment the President revoked the exile order and made plans to institute normal judicial proceedings against the three. But motivated perhaps by news which reached Santiago at the end of June that the junta in Seville had fallen and that in Buenos Aires the Viceroy had been deposed and a national junta created, García Carrasco ordered Ovalle, Rojas, and Vera shipped to Lima. While Vera lay ill in Valparaíso, Rojas and Ovalle sailed on July 10. Word of the deportation reached Santiago the following morning and occasioned general indignation. The *cabildo* met and, in recognition of the importance of the situation and the number of interested citizens who filled the streets, converted itself into a *cabildo abierto*—an open session, which all leading residents could attend. The *cabildo* in sisted that the President revoke his order, and after the Audiencia took a similar stand García Carrasco did rescind his instructions. But by this time Ovalle and Rojas were on the high seas. It was merely a short while before the Santiago population was aware of its failure.

Fearful that the President would take repressive measures against those who had instigated the movement for repeal of the order, a group of leading local residents formed themselves into a vigilante organ and resolved to protect themselves and their neighbors. The idea was attractive; almost overnight the civilian population of Santiago assumed a martial posture, even winning support from several influential military officers. Rather than chance revolution, the Audiencia requested that García Carrasco resign. This he did on July 16. The position devolved upon Brigadier Mateo de Toro Zambrano, Conde de la Conquista. Born in Santiago and well over eighty years old, Mateo de Toro Zambrano was one of Chile's most prominent landowners. His promotion to the rank of brigadier only the year before was no doubt inspired by the Crown's desire to secure his allegiance. He seemed an excellent choice for the presidency. Not only was he the highest ranking military official, but he was held in great esteem by his fellows, and he was a Chilean. But the tense situation proved to be more than he could handle.

No longer was it merely a question of loyalty to Ferdinand. The spectrum of choice shifted to the left: Now it was a question of loyalty to Ferdinand or the creation of a national junta in the example of the Viceroyalty of La Plata (whose capital was Buenos Aires), and one might argue, in the example of Spain itself. After all, the colonies belonged to the Crown, not to Spain. If the patriots in the mother country formed a junta to govern in the name of the deposed King, then it was only logical, to some at least, to do the same thing in Chile. The problem polarized Chile into two broad political groups, each with a vocal head. Leading the drive for a national junta was the *cabildo* of Santiago. The junta would be established in the name of Ferdinand. The Audiencia led the struggle for a continuation of the present governmental machinery in the name of Ferdinand.

The patriots in Spain complicated the matter. There the junta was superseded by a Council of Regency, recently established at Cádiz as a more effective instrument of carrying out the reconquest against the French. And the new President of Chile recognized the Regency. Thus it is probably with some chagrin that both he and the Audiencia read the instructions from the Regency calling for a Chilean deputy to attend a *Cortes*—legislative assembly—that was to convene at Cádiz. The instructions made it quite evident that the Regency considered it necessary to establish a program of political reform. This overt recognition of the need to reform the colonial system further fired the imagination of the Chilean patriots who desired a national junta.

Less than two months after he assumed the presidency, the situation deteriorated to such a point that Mateo de Toro Zambrano feared open warfare. To avert an internecine conflict, the President called for a *cabildo abierto* to meet on September 18. Several hundred people attended and voted for the creation of a national junta. The Junta was licensed to be but a provisional body, to function until a national assembly could convene. The exact pattern established in Spain was copied: first a provisional governing organ and then an assembly. Historians have not agreed about the nature of Chile's first national Junta, whether its creation implied that a decisive step toward independence had been taken. The *cabildo abierto* elected Mateo de Toro Zambrano President of the Junta. For Vice-President José Antonio Martínez, Bishop-elect of Santiago, was selected. The body of the Junta was supposed to comprise three *vocales*. First *vocal* was Fernando Márquez de la Plata, born in Spain to a distinguished family, and in his own right a prominent government official. Juan Martínez de Rozas was elected second *vocal*. For third *vocal* the *cabildo abierto* chose Ignacio de la Carrera, a leading landowner from Santiago. No plans had been made for additional members, but the general sentiment favored the election of two more *vocales*. Consequently, over four hundred people voted a second time during the same *cabildo abierto* and elected Francisco Javier Reina and Juan Enrique Rosales. The former was a Colonel of Artillery and a fervent supporter of the old regime. The latter was elected to represent the powerful Larraín family, to which he belonged by marriage, whose enormous size and influence permitted it to be in itself a political grouping called the *ochocientos*.

One could hardly consider the Junta a radical body. Pains were obviously taken to assure both the Regency and Ferdinand that a very respectable movement was under way. Only the views of Rozas might be held suspect, but he was elected, in part at least, to insure the loyalty of Concepción. The Junta had to swear to defend Chile to the last drop of blood in the name of Ferdinand VII, "to conserve and guard over our religion and laws; to provide justice"; and to recognize the Regency as the representative of the Crown. It is true that several leading Chileans considered the establishment of the Junta more than just an unusual event, that they perceived in it a major indication that independence could be a reality in the near future; but the overwhelming majority of the active citizenry either saw in the Junta the means of preserving the empire intact under pressures for reform, or saw in it the means of achieving reform without destroying the empire, which—though two distinctly different points of view—amounted to the same thing. It is only in the immediate years after 1810 that a viable, potent popular sentiment developed in support of independence, and only after it was declared did it become stylish to refer to September 18, 1810, as the first step toward independence. Chile began to govern itself in 1810 and for this privilege fought a war with the Viceroyalty of Peru in 1813. It was during these three years that Chileans cultivated an avid predilection for self-government.

• • •

The *cabildo* of Los Angeles was not informed officially of the establishment of the national Junta until the middle of November. It immediately swore allegiance to the governing body in Santiago. Several prominent members of the *cabildo* were related to O'Higgins. The *alcalde* was Francisco Riquelme, and the attorney was Simón Riquelme. Of the ten local residents who attended the meeting at which allegiance was announced, another was a Riquelme and one was O'Higgins himself.[6] The Los Angeles *cabildo* was the original font of O'Higgins' subsequent power.

As he told it a short while later, the "revolution of last September" found O'Higgins in the position of *subdelegado,* or civil governor, of La Laja, a post to which he was elected by the *cabildo* of Los Angeles. Previously, *subdelegados* were appointed by the Intendants: The colonial structure already was in transition before September 1810. It is quite interesting and revealing that O'Higgins referred to the establishment of the national Junta as a revolution. The liberty of Chile, he wrote in 1811, had been the "essential object of my thought and that which occupied the primary anxiety of my spirit, since in the year 1798 General Miranda inspired me." He was surprised that he had not been placed in jail along with two of his friends during the recent threat of an English invasion. "The moment that I knew of the deposition of Carrasco, I consulted with don Pedro Benavente, at that time military commander of Los Angeles, with respect to the convenience of taking measures that would assure our liberty, organizing in the province of Concepción the necessary forces; I committed myself to doing what was necessary to obtain such a goal on the Island of la Laja." Benavente approved his proposition so he proceeded with his "operations, and as a base for these, I took an approximate census of the inhabitants of the Island."

Thus he deduced that he could raise two good regiments of cavalry, leaving it up to Los Angeles to form a battalion of infantry. Having organized the two regiments, he so informed the Junta, and at the same time offered his own services, "but without soliciting any rank, since I was convinced that my old friend don Juan Rozas would proceed in justice and would name me Colonel of the number 2 regiment of la Laja, that that was composed of my own workers and those from the near vicinity." O'Higgins felt that he had deceived himself, "because our friend Doctor Rozas, in spite of his excellent qualities (and few men possess them in greater degree), was not free from domestic influences." A relative of Rozas', "Antonio Mendiburu, who did not have a single *cuadra* [square] of property in la Laja, was named Colonel of the regiment, and I Lieutenant Colonel."

The provisional Junta, "in the name of His Majesty señor don Fernando VII," confirmed O'Higgins in the rank of Lieutenant Colonel of the Second Regiment of Cavalry of the island of La Laja on February 28, 1811.[7] But he knew of the appointment over a month before the final confirmation. "I cannot hide my mortification upon seeing that an official without sufficient credentials was ranked higher than I, by a man whom I love and respect as a father." It was more than an emotional rebuff; it was a threat to his prestige in his home community. "My first impulse upon seeing myself thus slighted by a friend so loved, was to sell my livestock, rent my hacienda and proceed to Buenos Aires to fight as a volunteer. . . ." To further his point: "There I had no lands and, consequently, no credentials with which to expect any post; and I could not be treated with injustice."

But soon the task at hand took precedence over personal feelings. "But these sentiments of irritation . . . did not last a long time." Thinking about the matter in retrospect, he concluded that although he had appreciated the potential loss of local prestige, his real motivation had been his "damaged vanity." The rank of Lieutenant Colonel quickly began to appear to him adequate enough "to distinguish myself in the day of battle; and I came to believe that my post was high enough in order to serve my country." The agricultural phase of his life had lost its appeal. Membership in the local militia need not have filled him with a broader aspiration. By January of 1811 he was clearly concerned with a future outside La Laja. Even the rank of Lieutenant Colonel, he came to believe, "can be advantageous for me; it lessens in great part my responsibility during combat and, what is more important, it will stimulate me to rise higher in my career." But we cannot yet be sure of what career he was speaking.

While O'Higgins adjusted his personality to the vagaries of the new national situation, especially as it affected the frontier, the Junta in Santiago was confronted with some problems of its own. There were no political parties in Chile in September 1810, but there were political groupings, which by the end of the year possessed enough coherent unity to warrant the title of party. Not in the modern sense, however, since they were not formally organized on a year-round basis, with intricate programs and paid professional staffs, but parties they were nevertheless, by virtue of their power to seat or unseat governments, legally or otherwise. By the time the Junta was established, the active Chilean citizenry was divided into three general categories. The royalists opposed any move in the direction of independence. A sizable number of royalists were in fact Creoles who for various reasons were addicted to the colonial system. Then there was a rather large moderate group who desired a Chilean government of national origin tied to Ferdinand as a sovereign in a vague relationship probably not unlike a commonwealth. The last and most active group were the patriots who were determined to strike out for complete independence.[8] There existed greater variance of opinion among the patriots than among any other group. Though all three had at least two years in which to contemplate the eventuality of a national junta, not one proffered a plan of government by which the September Junta could operate.

However, Juan Egaña was quick to set down his ideas on paper. Just over forty years of age, Egaña was already one of Chile's most influential political theorists, and would eventually establish himself as the country's most noted writer of constitutions. His 1810 plan of government called for a modified system of free trade. The Crown had adopted measures of free trade in 1778, but these were not always welcome: Local products and manufactures often found it impossible to compete with foreign goods. Thus, according to Egaña's plan free trade would be adopted only where it was clear that the economy of the country would benefit. A decree of February 11, 1811, reflected this attitude precisely. A broad policy of free trade was adopted, but in conjunction with a provision to allow the enactment of rules, limitations, and restrictions necessary to "foment the industry of the country." [9] Egaña suggested that the Junta complete the Maipo Canal, just outside Santiago, construct roads to facilitate local commerce, and encourage domestic industry. He did not treat of the imposing problem of overproduction and domestic underconsumption. Nor did he envision the impending break with Lima and the subsequent termination of commercial traffic with the Pacific entrepôt.[10] Egaña's political program was far less specific. He spoke merely of a good government, with good heart and good advisers. An honest administration of justice would end countless evils. And, with surprising lack of prescience, he suggested that it was necessary to increase the present number of armed forces only a little in order to maintain public order.[11] Even had there not been an invasion from Peru in 1813, a great many more soldiers would have been required to confront both rebels and bandits.

Regardless of these intrinsic shortcomings, the first Junta at least had some sort of program to follow. All the various government corporations, such as the commercial and ecclesiastical tribunals, except for the Audiencia, swore allegiance to the Junta upon its establishment. The *oidores*—judges—of the Audiencia did not officially recognize the new government, but on September 19 they pledged their allegiance to Mateo de Toro Zambrano at his home. By the end of September the Junta was the generally uncontested governing body in Chile. Its greatest inadequacy was the absence of a firm leader who could command the respect of the population. Mateo de Toro Zambrano was largely a figurehead until his death at the end of February 1811. Bishop Martínez de Aldunate was also a less than virile leader. He died in early April 1811. The remaining members were either not greatly interested or were characteristically submissive. The situation changed abruptly with the arrival in Santiago of Juan Martínez de Rozas on November 2, 1810. By sheer energy and intellectual capacity Rozas would have been the paramount figure in the Junta; but in addition he was the most experienced Chilean bureaucrat in the Junta, the only one who had openly supported and helped achieve a national junta, and the only one who clearly represented an entire province. By the end of November Rozas in a very real sense was governing Chile with near-dictatorial powers.

Before leaving Concepción to take his place in the Junta, Rozas had a long private conference with O'Higgins "about the means that were necessary to adopt in order to assure the progress of the revolution and to promote the felicity of the country. . . ." As O'Higgins recalled, "I insisted strongly on two objects that were of vital interest in order to jolt the inertia of the Kingdom [*Reino*] and to launch the inhabitants on the path of revolution." There is no doubting O'Higgins' political orientation by January 1811 when he wrote the letter from which these quotations are taken. "These objects were the convocation of a Congress and freedom of commerce." But Rozas seemed to nourish doubts about the propriety of a congress just then, and upon reflection O'Higgins tended to agree. It is difficult to tell whether he made the following observation to Rozas at the time of the conference or it developed between that time and the writing of the letter. In any event, it indicates his attitude toward parliamentary government in the years prior to his own rise to power. It seemed to him "indubitable that the first Congress of Chile is going to give example of the most puerile ignorance and be criminal of every kind of folly. . . . Such consequences are inevitable in our present situation, lacking, as we do, every kind of skill and knowledge." Yet he agreed that a start had to be made. "But it is necessary to commence sometime, and the quicker that be, the greater advantages we will obtain." So dedicated was O'Higgins to the convocation of a congress that he chanced an open break with his mentor. He told Rozas that he should convoke a congress or resign, and if not, "far from counting on my cordial adhesion, he would find in me the most manifest hostility." If this was not rhetoric for a letter composed after the fact, O'Higgins distinctly exhibited a strength of character rather remarkable for a man whose adhesion in 1810 was not a very marketable item.

Upon his arrival in Santiago, Rozas was confronted by more critical problems than the question of a congress. One of his first acts was to adopt a plan for the military defense of the realm. The plan was drawn up by Captain of Engineers Juan Mackenna. Born near Dublin in 1771, Mackenna served Ambrosio Higgins in Peru as a military engineer. In 1797 the Viceroy named him political governor of Osorno so that he could better supervise the reconstruction of that region, long disturbed by natural catastrophes and Indian uprisings. In 1809 he married into the aristocratic Larraín family. The *cabildo* of Santiago on October 26, 1810, charged him with the task of preparing for the defense of Santiago. A three-man commission reviewed the plan and approved it late in November. Juan Egaña was one of the commissioners who agreed to Mackenna's proposals, which called for the raising of a militia of twenty-five thousand men to be divided into three great corps, and who obviously altered his previous position favoring a limited military organization.

The call for the national Congress was not made until December 15. The convocation decree stated that representatives of the entire realm were to meet in Santiago to decide upon the system that best suited its "regimen and security and prosperity during the absence of the king." The representatives would dictate rules for the different authorities and determine their duration and faculties. Since they were to face such a grave responsibility, representatives should be selected from among those individuals who, "through their enlightenment, probity, patriotism and talents, have merited the confidence and estimation of their fellow citizens. . . ." This does not appear at first very restrictive. Even more, the "Congress is a body representative of all the inhabitants of this kingdom. . . ." What is most impressive about this document is that the Junta in the name of Ferdinand was going to permit Chileans, also in the name of Ferdinand, to create any type of government they deemed appropriate. And equally remarkable, the Junta probably believed, to the limits of its own concepts, that the Congress to meet in Santiago would be truly representative.

Representation was declared to be proportional according to the population in each of Chile's twenty-five *partidos*—districts. Each district was to be allowed one Deputy except Concepción (3) Santiago (6), Chillán (2), Talca (2), and Coquimbo (2). To be a Deputy one had to be more than twenty-five years of age, but did not necessarily need to be a resident of the district from which he was elected. But the decree did state that, owing to the government's lack of financial resources, only those who could afford to pay their own expenses should be elected. This was not a devious means of eliminating most of the population; no one seemed concerned about the possible election of a domestic servant, for instance. It was merely a realistic approach to a seemingly insoluble problem. To vote in the election, one had to enjoy some importance by means of his fortune, position, talents or character, and be more than twenty-five years old. Restricted from the franchise were foreigners, the bankrupt, those indicted for crimes, those who had suffered a defamatory punishment, and those in debt to the royal treasury. So far as democracy is concerned, one need note only that the lists of eligible voters were drawn at the provincial level. There was little fear that the decree might be misinterpreted. The Congress was supposed to meet on April 15, 1811, and to begin its sessions on May 1.[12]

By early January 1811 provincial Chile was earnestly involved in the election of its Deputies. Shortly before he was elected Deputy from Los Angeles, O'Higgins wrote to Mackenna: "I have already passed the Rubicon. It is now too late to retreat, even if I desired, though I have never vacillated. I have enlisted under the colors of my country after the most judicious reflection, and I can assure you that never shall I repent, whatever be the consequences." But this is not to say that he was dissatisfied with the bucolic life. "The career to which I seem inclined by instinct and character, is that of a laborer. I owe to the generosity of the best of fathers a good education, solid moral principles and the conviction of the primordial importance that work and honesty have in the merit of man." And his health was now robust. "In such conditions I could have come to be a good campesino and a useful citizen and, would I have had the luck of being born in Great

Britain or in Ireland, I would have lived and died in the country." Considering his future place in Chilean affairs, this was a disconcertingly perceptive analysis of his own capabilities. As Supreme Director his most positive attributes would be solid moral principles, an eagerness to work hard, and an enviable honesty. In the country these, as he understood, would have been substantial credentials; but public administration was something else again. "But I have breathed for the first time in Chile and I cannot forget what I owe to my country. . . ." Surely many another patriot found himself in a similar predicament.

The purpose of O'Higgins' lengthy letter to Mackenna was to solicit military advice. He asked Mackenna to become his military tutor. "Do not believe . . . that I have the foolish vanity of aspiring to the role of a great military chief." The emphasis about what he did not aspire to become was on the word "great," not on "military chief." He expected to become a military chief, possibly even a general. It is clear that O'Higgins believed that a war would be necessary to continue the movement to which he referred as revolution, and to secure independence. This was entirely contrary to the point of view espoused recently by Juan Egaña in Santiago, and would have found little support among the royalists or moderates. Even for a patriot his seems to have been an extreme view. Here too he recognized his limitations. "I am convinced that the talents which constitute the great generals, like the great poets, must be born with us, and I am discerning enough to know that I lack these . . . ." He did not, he wrote, entertain the chimerical hope of some day being a great general; he knew his limitations and wanted to make the greatest effort to remedy the situation as much as possible. Thus he asked for instruction. One need not search too deeply to come away with the impression that he did in fact desire to be a great general. But his opinion of himself and great generals was all too accurate; his only claim to later fame as one would be his title.

Mackenna sent a letter of advice toward the end of February. A soldier, O'Higgins was told, should start his career right at the beginning, as a cadet; but since he had arrived at a jump almost at the top of the scale, he ought to supplement for study that which he would be able to learn in the field. He should seek out the sergeant of dragoons with the best reputation as an instructor: "With him you will quickly learn the use of the carbine, of the sword and of the lance and the exercise of cavalry and infantry in which your father customarily trained his own regiment." Then he should mount a horse and practice handling the sword and lance, and when this was learned sufficiently he could gather a company from his regiment for instruction exercises, with himself helping the sergeant at the task, "because in no way can you learn as well as by teaching others." After the movements of a company were mastered, he should call to his side an intelligent officer of dragoons and begin working with a squadron. This was critical because "only when you command it perfectly, will you be in a position to direct the entire regiment without danger of losing the estimation of the soldiers through some demonstration of ignorance." Every soldier, said Mackenna, must believe that you know more than he. That meant he must familiarize himself with every job in the regiment.[13] One can assume that O'Higgins was a willing student, since he later led troops in battle with some degree of skill.

However, it is certain that he did not practice military skills in the early months of 1811. Before the Mackenna letter arrived at Canteras, O'Higgins was elected Deputy to the national Congress from Los Angeles. The January 10, 1811 election named José María Benavente his alternate.[14] The instructions drawn by the *cabildo* for its representatives echoed the Junta's convocation decree rather closely. To comply with the instructions, O'Higgins was granted "the most efficacious and absolute power . . . ."[15] And, as it turned out, he believed this.

Most other *cabildos* elected their Deputies with as little hesitation or complication. But this was not to be so in Santiago, where the *cabildo* decided on January 8 that, based on the convocation decree's policy of proportional representation, it should send twelve Deputies rather than six. The *cabildo* concluded that if Concepción was permitted three Deputies, Santiago, merely on the basis of population, should have twelve. Purely on a mathematical principle it would have been impossible to contest this line of reasoning. On the basis of population, Santiago should have been allowed at least four times the number of Deputies elected by Concepción. Elections were set for May 6, but they were carried out two days earlier.[16] And this was done with full knowledge that the Congress was supposed to commence sessions on May 1.

While elections were being held in the provinces, Rozas was busy attempting to establish a solid foundation in Santiago for whatever national government the Congress would create. In this he was aided greatly by a short-lived military revolt in the capital led by Spanish Lieutenant Colonel Tomás de Figueroa. The fighting started on the first of April, and on the following day

Figueroa was executed. Rozas accused the Audiencia—the last important seat of royalist sentiment—of complicity in the revolt, and a short while later it was disbanded. Then with sure political instinct he announced that all Deputies-elect would be added to the Junta, to form a Superior Tribunal of Government. It was a brilliant strategic maneuver, at once making the Deputies party to his own administration and allaying fears that the Junta might try to maintain itself in power regardless of the wishes of Congress.

Early in May those Deputies now elected were installed officially as part of the governing tribunal, which soon took the name Superior Junta of Government. Rozas divided the Junta into three bodies: Royal Treasury, War, and Government and Police. O'Higgins served in the department of War.[17] Thus were established the prototypes of the future ministries. The Superior Junta governed until the installation of Congress on July 4. One of its most important acts was the creation of a Court of Appeals in June to replace the Audiencia. Unlike its predecessor, which enjoyed administrative privileges also, the Court was permitted only judicial functions.

The Congress was composed of several distinct groups. O'Higgins recognized the existence of three. First, there was the party of the *Godos*—the Spaniards. Many of these came from either Santiago or Concepción. Though they were in the minority they possessed power enough to restrict the actions of the patriots. Second, in the order that O'Higgins once listed them, were the *Indiferentes,* whom one might call the moderates. Since their vote often decided significant issues, their influence was greater even than their respectable number would indicate. Third was the party of the *Patriotas.* They gave impulse to what O'Higgins had referred to as the "revolution." Total independence from Spain and reform of the colonial system were their chief goals.[18] It is interesting that historian Diego Barros Arana placed only twelve Deputies in the patriot group, while O'Higgins listed twenty.[19]

Several features of the first Congress are of the utmost importance for an understanding of the independence era. Among the Deputies were several *mayorazgos,* titled aristocrats, and ecclesiastics. According to O'Higgins' categorization of the Deputies, it appears that the relationship between background and political viewpoint does not suggest a recognizable pattern. Deputies with similar backgrounds were in opposing political groups. Also interesting is that the leader of the patriot group, Rozas, was not elected a Deputy. Nor was Juan Egaña a Deputy until a special election in November was held. And the election of one of the most celebrated advocates of a national junta, Camilo Henríquez, was disputed, with the result that he never became a Deputy. In addition to Egaña there was one other highly respected theoretician, Manuel de Salas. Deputy from Itata, Salas was born in Santiago in 1754 and educated at the University of San Marcos in Lima. In 1779 he went to Spain to complete his education and remained there for about five years. Ambrosio Higgins marked his return home by naming him superintendent of public works. In 1795 the Crown appointed him syndic of the *consulado,* and two years later he became Director of the prestigious Academy of San Luis. In Congress he aligned with the patriots. Two of the groups in Congress had rather uncomplicated tasks: The *Godos* merely had to maintain the status quo, and the moderates, requiring just slightly more political dexterity, had to referee the contest between the two extreme groups. Since the patriots were the ones who desired change, it was they who had to be the innovators. Outside Congress they could rely on the enlightened counsel of Rozas, and within there were Salas and Father Juan Pablo Fretes, who had known O'Higgins in Spain. These were men who understood the need for reform, but could call to their support only vague theoretical ideas concerning an appropriate political system. Though they had read and discussed the very best of the European Enlightenment both in Chile and abroad, they had received no tutoring in adjusting theory to reality. This is not to say that the early leaders lacked ability to administrate, for in this they had been trained and in this they demonstrated considerable competence. One should not confuse, as some writers have done, the ability to create an effective government with the ability to govern effectively.

Juan Antonio Ovalle was elected President of the Congress at the first session. Ovalle, one of those arrested by García Carrasco, and a *mayorazgo,* figured among the moderates. The pleasantries of a session of installation were disrupted when twelve Deputies presented the Congress a formal protest against the seating of Santiago's additional six representatives. The protest stated that every province that had elected Deputies according to the convocation decree was legally free from obeying the decisions of Congress. It was not an auspicious beginning for Chile's first legislature. O'Higgins was one of those who signed the protest.[20] No action was taken by Congress for the moment.

The protest was left in abeyance probably because neither side was all too sure how to go about running a legislature. There existed no established procedure by which the Congress could conduct its business. It was decided at the outset that sessions would convene between ten in the morning and two in the afternoon. Though many delegates—including those from Santiago, who were among the few with precise instructions from a *cabildo* —favored open sessions, the Deputies chose to meet in secrecy. After two months, however, the sessions were opened to the public. But more problematic was the question of the very nature of the body. It was clear to all deputies that the Congress was a legislature, but many assumed that it was also supposed to be an executive body. Thus, all during July the Congress had to spend much time administering minor business. By the end of the month the Deputies decided to elect a new three-man junta with a rotating president, but the plan did not come to a vote.

By the beginning of August procedural problems had been worked out, and the Congress settled down to more significant matters. On August 5 Manuel Pérez de Cotapos was elected the new President of Congress, and Juan Cerdán was elected Vice-President. Both were, surprisingly, *Godos;* the influence of the patriots was obviously waning. The following day it was voted to refuse a request from the Spanish Regency for financial support. O'Higgins was one of the most vehement in opposition to the sending of funds.[21] It is likely that he, as well as many of his patriot colleagues, feared that such an act would suggest that the Regency had justly assumed Crown privileges over the colonies. And, on the other hand, it is probable that all groups in Congress appreciated that Chile could not financially afford to support the Regency or even establish such a precedent.

On August 7 the question of a new junta was again considered, but no agreement was reached and Congress was threatened with a deadlock. The following day Manuel de Salas proposed that the thirty Deputies from the province of Santiago be permitted to elect two members to the junta, and the twelve from Concepción the additional member. This would have given the patriots one man on the junta: Rozas. The plan was appealing to many Deputies, but it did not include the north. Patriot Deputy from Valparaíso Augustín Vial suggested that the northern districts, including Valparaíso, be allowed to elect a fourth member to the junta. But majority sentiment remained in favor of a three-man junta. By the beginning of the second week of August the patriots came to the decision that they would not be able to control a new junta. And on August 9 the twelve Deputies who had signed the protest against Santiago's self-enlarged deputation walked out of Congress in a group. This left the legislature in the hands of the *Godos* and moderates. An extraordinary session was called for the following morning, a Sunday. Without opposition the Deputies elected Martín Calvo Encalada, Juan José de Aldunate and Francisco Javier del Solar to comprise the new Junta. Solar was to represent Concepción, but was not at the time in Santiago. In his place, as an alternate, Juan Miguel Benavente was elected.[22]

Chile's second executive Junta was very much unlike its predecessor. Congress reserved the right to control patronage over the Church, traditionally an executive function, and to conduct foreign relations. Management of the army, including the appointment of all officers, pertained to the Congress as well. To further enfeeble the Junta, the Congress allowed itself the privilege of reviewing all its acts. The Junta was commissioned to function until the promulgation of a constitution or the termination of a year, whichever came first. Not only was the Junta without power to act with certainty and provide the executive leadership mandatory for stability and progress, but the prominent patriots, among whom there were several with executive ability, no longer were active in government. Rozas was out of a job, and he made plans to return to Concepción. Deputies such as Fretes, Salas, and O'Higgins were not attending the congressional sessions. It is this situation which made possible the meteoric rise to power of José Miguel Carrera and the naming of a new junta in September.

Once they removed themselves from Congress, the several maverick Deputies from Concepción addressed a circular to their electors justifying their recent stand. The essence of the argument was that the plan for a junta would render all districts of Chile "subject to the caprice of the capital and reduced to a degrading inferiority." [23] O'Higgins made a similar statement in Santiago to the residents of Los Angeles. He had hoped that a plan would be adopted to elect a junta "representative of the populace or, at least, of the three departments of the kingdom, comprised of this capital, of Concepción and of Coquimbo. . . ." But in all his efforts for an equitable solution he failed, and thus he decided to separate himself from the Congress.[24]

For their part, the remaining Deputies did not stay silent. The Congress directed a circular to the provinces cogently arguing the validity of the three-man Junta. And this it did well. The central theme of the circular was that each Deputy had been elected by the various *cabildos* to act not by himself but in union with the other Deputies who had received equal power. Thus it was impossible, the Congress averred, for one province to determine legislation. In theory this was so: The Deputies, after all, were not elected by province. Even in reality there was justification for such a position: The twelve absent Deputies did not come all from the same province. And at any rate, the *cabildo* of Santiago had requested approval from the national Junta for the election of the six additional representatives, and the Junta agreed. The *cabildo* had not acted illegally. The only basis for the walkout was that a minority of Deputies assured themselves that they could not elect a satisfactory junta. In closing, the circular called for a new vote to replace those Deputies not in attendance, with the stipulation that the same Deputies could be re-elected.[25]

And on August 13 a *cabildo abierto* in Los Angeles elected O'Higgins its Deputy once again. In place of Benavente, who was in Buenos Aires, Gaspar Marín was chosen alternate. The *cabildo* reaffirmed O'Higgins' powers, "but under the express condition of not entering into any further negotiations with the six deputies designated by the most excellent junta of the capital of Santiago. . . ." The *cabildo* also approved the protest that O'Higgins had signed.[26]

Though a Deputy to Congress once again, and still residing in Santiago, O'Higgins did not immediately attend the sessions. By the middle of August he was seriously stricken with a bronchial condition and confined to his bed. It was for this reason that he did not accompany Rozas to Concepción as he had planned. In fact, he remained physically inactive for about two months. And this was a period when it would have been in his interest to be active and have Rozas at his side in Santiago.

While Congress was in session on September 4, 1811, José Miguel Carrera presented it with what was to become his famous petition in the name of the people of Santiago. Carrera might easily be considered the most interesting character of the entire independence movement in Chile. Born in Santiago in 1786, he had only arrived back home from his study trip to Spain at the end of July. Before he was twenty-six he controlled the government of Chile. Several factors contributed to this. Carrera's father, Ignacio de la Carrera, was descended from the early conquistadores and a member of one of Chile's most aristocratic families. Carrera's brothers, Juan José and Luis, were military officers in control of key forces. José Miguel himself had earned a distinguished reputation as an officer in the Spanish army. Perhaps most important in establishing the personal charisma that contrived to render people susceptible to his political machinations was the already mentioned absence of a dynamic personality to lead Chile out of the pointless calm which fell upon the colony by the end of August. All things taken together, José Miguel Carrera, of a good family, a soldier, brash, not lacking in *sang-froid,* was an attractive young man.

Physically intimidated by Carrera, the Congress remained in session way into the night and before adjourning complied with most of his demands. The delegation from Santiago was reduced to six members. Several Deputies were removed from Congress and exiled to the provinces. Even several military officers and municipal officials lost their positions through congressional decree. The most important event of the long evening was the establishment of a five-man Junta to govern for three years. Carrera not only stipulated the number but also the names: Juan Enrique Rosales, Juan Martínez de Rozas, Martín Calvo Encalada, Juan Mackenna, and Gaspar Marín. Officially, Carrera held no position in the new government, but the members of the Junta understood well that they owed their jobs to him. Rozas never sat in the Junta, and was replaced shortly by Juan Miguel Benavente. Carrera obviously intended to give the Junta a broader base of support than it had enjoyed previously. For the first time the powerful Larraín family was represented, now in the person of Mackenna and Rosales. Concepción got Rozas, and the northern districts Gaspar Marín, who was connected with the town of La Serena.

However much Carrera may have intended to mollify provincial reaction to the altered government, not everyone was impressed. The *cabildo* of Concepción created its own Junta for the entire province. Local municipalities immediately began to recognize and swear allegiance to it. The *cabildo* of Los Angeles did this on September 17, even swearing to obey its orders.[27] The proliferation of juntas was certainly going to lessen the effectiveness of the central government. Yet if a new junta could be established in Santiago, the provinces seemed justified in creating their own, much in the example of the first Spanish and Chilean juntas. Los Angeles itself contemplated establishing one. This O'Higgins applauded vigorously. Local juntas should be looked upon "as unshakable columns of the liberty of the country, and a firm support of the rights of the provinces. . . ." [28]

While the provinces and the capital were in the process of invoking a final confrontation, the Carrera-inspired Congress proceeded to produce a commendable record. Though he was in Santiago, O'Higgins was still ill and did not attend the sessions until after the middle of October. The Congress gave high priority to the insidious relationship that traditionally existed between the parish priest and his flock. On September 24 the Deputies passed a law abolishing payment for marriage, baptism, and several other common priestly services. The Congress would study means of indemnifying the parishes for the loss of income. This was congressional legislation and did not require Junta approval. To better gauge how to repay the parishes, the Congress later took steps to ascertain the average quinquennium income of the episcopates. To assure greater accuracy, the Deputies also called for a report on the state of the *diezmo*—the church tithe. Since meager financial resources acted as a stricture upon the expansive plans of Congress, it is more than likely that the Deputies appreciated the value of such lists should a policy of direct taxation ever be desirable. On the same day the Deputies ended all personal contributions of labor for the construction of churches.

By October the Congress was the center of progressive activity in Chile. The Junta remained in an awkward position: There existed no body of rules by which it could act, and its powers over the Concepción Junta were not clear. Early in October the Congress named a commission of five Deputies to formulate a provisional ordinance of the faculties of the executive Junta. Apart from the fact that such a clarification was necessary, the Deputies no doubt saw further opportunity to insure their primacy over the Junta. On the following day the Congress voted to admit the indigenous population to the state schools, on an equal basis with the "descendants of Spaniards. . . ."

The Congress was not concerned with domestic problems exclusively. Francisco Antonio Pinto, later to be President of Chile, was named representative (*diputado* as he was called officially) to the Junta of Buenos Aires. Thus Pinto became Chile's first diplomatic agent. On its part Buenos Aires already had sent an agent to Chile. It was decided to send two secret agents to Lima in order to inform the Viceroy of recent events. At the same session that diplomatic matters were treated the Congress voted to take a general census of the colony with the object of establishing the demarcation of provinces and fixing their representation in Congress.

By the second week of October the Congress seemed to be gaining its stride. On October 11 the Deputies voted that henceforth copies of all acts of Congress were to be made available to the public, "so that all the citizens can read them, demand their execution, criticize them, or make useful remarks about them." This was not a devious maneuver to conjure up a resemblance to liberal government, rather, it seems to have been an honest attempt to make the government of the active citizenry as liberal as the requirements of public order and safety would allow. Though the Deputies were not overly concerned with constitutional inequities, they were among the hemisphere's leaders in ending Negro slavery. Also on the eleventh they prohibited the introduction of new slaves into the realm and declared free all those who, in transit from other areas, might remain six months in Chile. Children born to slaves in the future were likewise declared free, even if their parents might leave Chile. The Deputies also recommended good treatment of those slaves who remained in Chile.

One of the more controversial reforms of the month had to do with public cemeteries. Traditionally, Chilean Catholics—and there were precious few of any other kind—were buried in sacred Church ground, preferably within the physical Church structure itself. Burial plots became a highly valued commodity, and traffic in them enhanced the economic and political position of the Church. But crowding and inadequate sanitary precautions threatened the health of urban centers. The movement for the creation of public cemeteries outside the centers of population was led in Congress by Father Fretes, perhaps the most democratically minded Deputy. O'Higgins was one of his chief allies in winning support for the measure, which came to a vote on October 18. The Congress, with O'Higgins in attendance for the first time since his re-election, voted to establish the cemeteries, and named a commission of three to supervise the founding of one for Santiago. So turbulent was the opposition to the measure that the first public cemetery was not created for a decade.

His two months of convalescence allowed O'Higgins sufficient time and quietude to think about his responsibilities as a provincial Deputy. By the time of his return to active membership he had formulated a plan for congressional action. He determined to ask for a law to allow the district of Los Angeles to use certain public lands for the benefit of the local school system. In frontier settlements, O'Higgins thought, political authority should not be placed in the hands of the military commander. Such combination of powers was not generally conducive to good government and improved local conditions along the frontier. He estimated that the island of La Laja held a population of at least twenty thousand people, but had only one priest. For this reason he planned to solicit the erection of a convent on the island. He thought the gunpowder factory in Los Angeles should be removed to the outskirts of the town to lessen the chance of a disastrous explosion. Los Angeles should be permitted to license eight general stores, since "a new population has many necessities." To protect the local economy, wines produced outside the district should not be allowed into the district until all Los Angeles wine be sold.[29] He also believed that the condition of the national army along the frontier was deplorable, with Los Angeles, "the capital of the frontier," supporting a military establishment of twenty to twenty-five non-militia soldiers. For the local cattle industry and agriculture to flourish, there must be protection by the national army against bandits and Indians.[30] He wanted more soldiers for the district.

Though not especially complex the plan indicates his intimate familiarity with the needs of provincial Chile. Even later, as Supreme Director, he demonstrated a perceptive appreciation of both local and national requirements, but the ability to produce results was indeed another matter. O'Higgins' views in 1811 offer an insight into his later actions once Supreme Director. The public school system must be supported, if only indirectly. An efficacious military establishment must be maintained, but where advisable its command should be separate, even under an uncertain frontier milieu, from local political authority. The local economy should be protected when necessary by restricting importation. Perhaps most interesting, considering his affinity for revolutionary ideas and his European experience, was his desire to place the Church in closer contact with the people. O'Higgins was not a democrat, but he was a liberal in the nineteenth-century sense of the term. When later Chileans would search the independence epoch for the roots of their modern democracy they would often settle upon José Miguel Carrera as their champion. Once Carrera entered politics, the patriot party became less monolithic. The group to which O'Higgins pertained could be called moderate and the Carreristas, radical.[31]

The Congress began to act on O'Higgins' proposals late in October. But before he could guide the entire program through the legislature he found it necessary to absent himself from the capital. On November 6 he solicited Congress for permission to return to the south for a period of convalescence. "After a fierce rheumatism that had me prostrate in bed more than two months and a half," a period of rest away from Santiago and the responsibilities of Congress was required. The application was approved immediately. Since he was going south anyway, the Congress commissioned him to referee the elections at Curicó, which had resulted in a dispute. One of the last acts of Congress before the creation of the fourth Junta was to appoint a commission to write a constitution to govern Chile "during the captivity of the king."

On November 15 the Carreras carried out their second successful *golpe de estado*. O'Higgins already had sent his baggage south, and at seven in the morning of that day mounted his horse for the trip to Curicó. But news that the Congress was being forced to vote in a new Junta caused him to wait out the result. Three *vocales* were elected to the Junta: Rozas for Concepción, José Miguel Carrera for Santiago, and Gaspar Marín for Coquimbo. O'Higgins was elected alternate for Rozas or *vocal* in the event that Rozas should not appear in Santiago. At eight-thirty in the evening of the following day O'Higgins was summoned before Congress and told of his election. "To this I answered that my health not being improved, I was not in a condition to discharge the office as I should. . . ." Moreover, right from the time he entered Congress, he observed, he had supported incessantly the representative system, in conformity with the wishes of his province. And since the people of Santiago did not have the right to elect representatives to the central government for the other provinces, the present procedure was illegal. He asked to be excused from representation on the Junta. The Congress replied that the present system was, in fact, representative and a Junta of three *vocales* conformed with the wishes of the Concepción Junta made known in a note received that same morning. And if O'Higgins should come to believe that the government was truly unrepresentative, he was told, he would not be forced to hold a position in it. At any rate, it was a provisional appointment that the province of Concepción could ratify. The Congress also took its previously voiced opinion that it possessed the legal right to act for the entire realm, especially on a provisional basis. According to O'Higgins, the Congress ended its persuasive argument by observing that his acceptance would serve to avert a possibly anarchical situation. This was just the right note on which to end. So, to avoid the evils of anarchy he accepted the position, but under the express condition that he would consult about the matter with the province of Concepción and retire from his post the moment it did not approve his representation of the province. At nine o'clock he was sworn in.[32]

Things were certainly moving with great celerity. Already on the sixteenth the Junta was issuing decrees. O'Higgins signed his name to a statement written by the Junta on the same day in which he officially became a *vocal*. Two days later the Congress granted it legal power as the executive agent of government.[33] Carrera was not satisfied with the new arrangement, and by the end of the month formulated plans for a further aggrandizement of power. Acting in conjunction with him, the military commanders in Santiago on December 2, 1811, presented Congress a note calling for its dissolution. According to the officers, they were acting under the orders of the sovereign public, whose will it was that the Congress suspend its sessions and invest the Junta with the three powers (executive, legislative, and judicial) of government. At first, the Congress agreed to suspend its sessions, but refused to transfer its powers. Carrera, supported by a substantial military contingent, insisted, and the Deputies quickly came around to his point of view. On the same day that the military note was presented, Congress disbanded and transferred all its powers to the Junta.[34]

On the third, the remaining powers of government devolved by default upon Carrera. *Vocal* Gaspar Marín presented what amounted to a resignation, and Carrera accepted it. O'Higgins did the same thing, and again Carrera accepted. By coincidence, it was on this same day that the Concepción Junta approved O'Higgins' acceptance of a position on the Junta in the first place.[35] O'Higgins gave poor health as the reason for his desired separation from government, but it is quite likely that he disapproved of Carrera's acquisitive actions. This put Carrera in a precarious position; O'Higgins' break with the government was now fact, yet his loyalty might be critical should there be a confrontation with Rozas. In the creation of a new government O'Higgins could be used as the representative of Concepción instead of Rozas, who was considerably less submissive to Carrera's demands. On December 4 Carrera sent notes to the provinces justifying the suspension of congressional sessions. To Concepción he asserted that the best means of governing Chile was a system of representation. Thus Chile had been divided into three provinces with each one sending a *vocal* to the central Junta. Since Rozas never took his seat in the Junta, and O'Higgins was only an alternate, the province was invited to elect another *vocal*.[36]

O'Higgins' potential usefulness became painfully evident to Carrera in a matter of days. Intercepted documents indicated that the province of Concepción was ready to go to war rather than allow Carrera to usurp power in Santiago. Once he was sure of the veracity of the intelligence he paid O'Higgins a personal visit, explained the situation, and asked him to proceed immediately to Concepción to make known his peaceful intentions, and as his representative, settle any points of disagreement between the province and the national Junta. On December 13, 1811, Carrera signed an order naming O'Higgins his secret envoy to Concepción. This was all characteristic of Carrera's studied arrogance. He was acting in the name of a Junta that in reality did not exist. The conciliatory gesture could only improve his position. Either Concepción would agree to the recent change in government, or he would at least have enough time to prepare his military forces for a conflict.

O'Higgins arrived in Concepción on December 27. The Junta received him cordially and appointed Fernández Vásquez de Novoa to negotiate with him in the name of the province. Others took part in the conferences, most notably Rozas. On January 12, 1812, a pact of twenty-five articles was signed by the two representatives. The first article stated that supreme authority resided in the Chilean people. And more, public officials were accountable to the people for their actions. It was agreed that the congressional sessions should remain suspended, unless it became necessary to adopt a permanent constitution. In such an event the Congress would have to convene. In the meantime, the government of Chile would be considered provisional, and composed of three *vocales,* who would be elected one by each province. The tenure of office for a *vocal* was set at not less than two years and not more than three years. It is not clear whether Concepción actually wanted the establishment of a Senate. The pact stated that the governing Junta would decide whether it was appropriate to create a six-member Senate, with each province sending two representatives.[37] The wording could have been more assertive. It seems that Rozas hoped for a Senate that would have to approve such major steps as the declaration of war or establishment of peace, the imposition of new taxes, the drawing of treaties with foreign powers or other American colonies, the promulgation of new laws or the revision of old ones, and the addition of personnel to the army.[38] Thus, it is surprising that the pact did not at least suggest that a Senate was desirable.

Perhaps the most interesting clause was the eleventh, which treated of the relationship between Chile and Spain. In no event was the Spanish *Cortes,* the Regency, or any other government instituted in Spain to be recognized, or any of its representatives admitted into Chile until Ferdinand VII be restored to his throne. This meant that, so far as contemporary Spain was concerned, Chile in effect was independent. Though not officially independent, Chile had been governing her own affairs for well over a year now. While Chileans had not generally agreed upon a form of government, they had been united in an effort to bring about reforms in the colonial system. The Congress of 1811 had in fact been progressive. By the end of the year most members of the active citizenry probably thought they were capable, once a stable apparatus was erected, of administering their own government. But by the beginning of 1812 Chileans had been unfettered too long to return impassively to the old colonial way of life merely upon the restoration of Ferdinand. Should he be returned to the throne, and Chile not already have declared independence, the pact stated, negotiations would be entered into in order to obtain freedom of trade and local manufactures, and so that the government of Chile would assume a new form, not remaining "as in the past exposed to the horrors of despotism and arbitrariness." The influence of O'Higgins and Rozas was quite evident here.

The Concepción Junta approved the pact on January 13, 1812, and sent it on to Santiago. Carrera received it on the twenty-first. From that moment he set a course of procrastination, the ratification of the pact being a decided threat to his power. He immediately called for a meeting of leading citizens to discuss the various issues. Far from taking an open stand against the pact, Carrera gave every indication that he was not deliberately wasting time, but, rather, was using it to insure an orderly and acceptable denouement. The Santiago Junta—still comprising only Carrera—sent O'Higgins two notes of congratulations and thanks for negotiating the pact.[39] In February he found additional excuses for not signing or rejecting it. For one thing, he had requested that the ecclesiastical tribunal present an opinion of the pact, and this was not received until early February. The religious tribunal stated that it would comment only on religious matters. It found two articles objectionable. The Spanish government, established in the name of Ferdinand, should be recognized. Also the clauses that reiterated the laws passed by the Congress of 1811 abolishing various parish fees should be eliminated.[40] Such things gave the Concepción Junta hope enough not to mobilize for war. After all, though a dictator, Carrera held progressive ideas and was keeping the peace. On February 13 the *Aurora de Chile,* the country's first newspaper, made its appearance. Though short-lived, lasting only to April 17, the *Aurora* championed liberal reform and independence from Spain. Through the efforts of editor Camilo Henríquez those literate Chileans yet unfamiliar with the basic concepts of the Enlightenment quickly became initiated. On the one hand, Carrera was not agreeing to a diminution of his powers, but on the other, he was giving the active citizenry cause to cheer his administration.

While the two Juntas—to borrow Carrera's euphemistic term—were cautiously avoiding a final showdown, O'Higgins remained in the south. Toward the end of January he was informed that the *cabildo* of Los Angeles had elected him *alcalde,* and that the provincial Junta had confirmed the decision. But O'Higgins declined to accept. During his absence of nearly a year in service to the realm, the hacienda had fallen into a state of disorder, and required his constant attention. He felt he could not devote as much time to the municipal position as it deserved. In February the Junta of Concepción conferred upon him the rank of Lieutenant Colonel of Army in recognition of his services as a congressional Deputy.[41] It was not unusual for Chilean governments, both provincial and central, to reward political services with military appointments.

By the beginning of March militia troops along the somewhat vague border between the provinces of Santiago and Concepción were activating under their own orders. To avert what was fast becoming inevitable, the Junta of Concepción met in conjunction with a *cabildo abierto* on March 7. Without a negative vote Colonel Luis de la Cruz was elected to proceed directly to Santiago to demand a definitive answer concerning the aging pact. Cruz was a member of Chile's first Junta, and one of the province's leading residents. At the same time the assembly took further military precautions. Without financial support from Santiago the province would have a rather difficult time financing a war effort. Consequently, O'Higgins was elected to represent the city of Concepción in canvassing the economic resources of the rest of the province and making arrangements with the other districts to finance a military action.[42] But he had no chance to become deeply involved in the project. On March 9 over a thousand troops under the command of Brigadier Juan José Carrera left Santiago for the south.

Word of the troop movement and the justification for it by the Santiago Junta reached Concepción five days later. The troops were called out at once, and Rozas, who had been made a brigadier by the Congress of 1811, was given command of all Concepción forces. On the same day, the fourteenth, O'Higgins was ordered to La Laja to take command, in the absence of a colonel, of his regiment and prepare it to march north.[43] Within days Concepción had several thousand soldiers under arms.[44] Then Carrera wrote another note stating that he had sent troops south only to counter the self-ordered activity of Concepción's border militia. The capital was not going to mount an act of aggression. Rather, it was a defensive movement. In response to the note, which seemed to justify Carrera's actions, the Concepción Junta ordered an immediate halt to the military buildup. The two capitals began sending notes back and forth. Carrera never approved the pact, but he also never made objections to any specific articles. It was Rozas who led the peace movement in Concepción. Others, however, opted for military action, especially in light of Concepción's superior military power. O'Higgins proposed a plan of action. The troops sent by Carrera were stationed on the northern bank of the Maule River, just to the south of Talca. They were not, he believed, well equipped or trained. O'Higgins proposed to lead a force of a thousand disciplined troops across the Maule, disperse the Santiago forces, and then proceed on to the relatively unguarded capital itself. It was a daring plan that won considerable support, even from several members of the Junta. But Rozas thought the military too eager, threw his prestige and power against it, and the plan was discarded. It did, however, serve to lessen the steadying influence of Rozas in revolutionary circles.

In early May the two provincial leaders both favored a meeting. They met at Talca and discussed possible solutions to the static situation. O'Higgins was often the messenger between the two when some ground rule had to be laid. Both sides agreed to the recalling of troops from the Maule—Rozas, because it was a gesture of peace, and Carrera, because he needed extra military support in Santiago. Yet the meetings actually decided little, and negotiations broke off on May 19. Carrera returned to Santiago, but Rozas and O'Higgins were caught by the seasonal rains at Linares, and there had to remain for several days. The humid weather doubtless caused O'Higgins considerable discomfort. From Canteras he wrote his mother at the end of May that she should tell people that an attack of rheumatism in a shoulder made it impossible for him to attend an assembly at Concepción called by Rozas to determine means of supporting the province economically, and especially of paying the troops. From the letter one gets the impression that in part this was an excuse to allow him to stay away from Concepción.

In the evening of July 8 Rozas found out how accurately he had gauged restlessness among the military. With only minor resistance, a military rebellion led by Juan Miguel Benavente, Ramón de Jiménez Navia, and José Zapatero dislodged the Concepción government from power. On the following morning a junta of war was created under the presidency of Pedro José Benavente. In September, Benavente dissolved the junta and declared himself Governor-Intendant. Since he and Carrera were in basic agreement, Chile was now more or less united—at least where it counted most, in the two major provinces. O'Higgins had nothing to do with these events. He spent much of his time at the thermal baths of Perquilauquen and did not return to Canteras until January 1813.

While Concepción was in the process of changing its government, Santiago endeavored to establish a more formal foundation for its administration. Influential in this was recently arrived United States Consul Joel Roberts Poinsett. A compulsive advocate of his country's form of government, Poinsett went out of his way to contact leading Chileans and convince them of the need for a constitution, and, in particular, one modeled on the United States example. He even drafted a constitution and presented it to Carrera in July. True to its precepts it called for an administration of three branches, with the executive being a *gran jefe*—a great chief. Not surprisingly, the Chilean counterpart of the United States President would be at least thirty-six years old. It is remarkable that Poinsett should display such little political acumen: Carrera was only twenty-eight at the time. The document was not accepted. However, many who had settled into a sort of *de facto* support of Carrera continued to press for a constitution. A provisional document was adopted on October 27.

It was a very short constitution that provided for nearly everything that Concepción had desired and Carrera had refused. The conciliatory gesture most certainly must have taken Concepción by surprise. A three-man Junta would enjoy the executive power. But it was a power very much restricted by a Senate of seven members. The provinces of Concepción and Coquimbo were allowed two representatives each, but Santiago would have three. The Junta required senatorial approval on all important matters, such as declaring war, effecting a peace, coining money, establishing alliances and treaties of commerce, naming envoys, moving troops from one point to another, increasing the number of troops, and altering the constitution. All faculties not expressly declared in the document were reserved to the sovereign public. There would be freedom of press, but so that this freedom would not degenerate into license, the Junta and Senate would prescribe rules of conduct.

Typical of the early Chilean liberal approach was Article 24, which stated that all free Chileans were equal before the law, with only merit and virtue rendering one individual more suitable for public office than another. Again, this was not an overt subterfuge designed to suggest a progressive outlook. It was indeed a sincere move. Individual members of the active citizenry no doubt considered merit and virtue not at all restrictive to their group as a whole. At this date in Chilean history it was not yet a question of whether a domestic servant possessed the characteristics requisite for office-holding. The constitution had to be approved by the provinces. The new administration would govern Chile in the name of Ferdinand VII.[45]

The constitutional government, with a Junta under the tutelage of its most powerful member, Carrera, began to function almost at once, and by the end of the year was in firm control. As the first months of 1813 passed, it appeared the political turbulence had exhausted itself, as though the ship of state had righted itself, and was sailing in the doldrums awaiting news of Ferdinand. Then came the invasion from Peru.

CHAPTER III

The Invasion from Peru

THOUGH THE GOVERNMENT OF CHILE STILL FUNCTIONED IN THE NAME of Ferdinand, it did not consider itself subservient to the present government of Spain, or consequently, to Viceroy Abascal of Peru. Thus the Viceroy sent an expedition under General Pareja to discipline the errant colony, and segments of the population chose to fight for the independence from Peru which they had known since 1810. Pareja landed at San Vicente, just south of the port of Talcahuano and north of Concepción, on March 27, 1813. In little more than a day the news reached O'Higgins at Canteras, and he quickly called out the militia of La Laja. In admirably short time he marched the troops directly for Concepción. On March 29 he was met by a soldier with orders from Intendant Benavente to disperse the troops and return to Canteras.

But O'Higgins refused to obey. Instead, he marched north to Talca, on the northern side of the Maule River, in the hope of offering resistance to the invaders to detain them long enough for reinforcements to arrive. Once past the Maule and Talca the enemy would have a choice of unobstructed paths into Santiago. He arrived at his destination on April 4. By that time Carrera, as commander of all Chilean forces, was also at Talca. On the very next day Colonel O'Higgins was ordered by Carrera to march immediately to deliver a verbal communiqué to Pareja. The written orders O'Higgins received indicated that the enemy must be made aware that the responsibility of a war would rest with the invader.[1] While O'Higgins was expediting the order, the Bishop of Santiago exhorted the residents and soldiers of Talca to join in the defense of the realm.[2] Even a radical patriot like Carrera appreciated the value of the Church at such a moment.

O'Higgins must have been extremely optimistic about the chances of successfully defending Chile. When he left Canteras at the end of March he allowed his mother and sister to remain at the hacienda, something he would hardly have done had he expected a lengthy fight. And it was an attitude that affected his military outlook. Before he departed from Talca, he informed

Carrera that during his march to the city he had learned that a small advance guard of the invasion forces was headed for Linares. He suggested to Carrera that since he was going south anyway, he should be given a few extra soldiers to meet the enemy and deal them an initial blow that would break their morale. Carrera did not at first approve, but after Consul Poinsett told Carrera that he supported the plan—an unusual role for a diplomat to essay—O'Higgins was given the troops. He arrived at Linares on April 6, charged the plaza and dispersed the enemy force, even taking several prisoners. This was the first battle of the war, and it was successful.

Though merely a skirmish, the battle at Linares motivated O'Higgins and his small force on to even greater deeds. He made his way farther south and secured Los Angeles and La Laja. Using his own funds he organized a division from his home district. By the middle of the Chilean winter, O'Higgins, without yet fighting a pitched battle of consequence, was fast becoming a popular military hero. But the notoriety did not always benefit him. While he was fighting away from home, the invaders took La Laja and destroyed Canteras. His family fled to Concepción, but were captured and taken to Chillán. This was the same city which O'Higgins had failed to capture just a short while before. By the spring of 1813 his romantic conception of war must surely have been dispelled. Though generally victorious, he had not yet won a major battle, his hacienda had been devastated, and his mother and sister had been taken prisoner.

Likewise, the central government came to understand the true nature of the conflict and its potential duration. On October 8 the Junta decided to move to Talca, so it might better prosecute the war effort. By decree it invested itself with all the extraordinary powers that it might ordinarily need senatorial approval to obtain.[3] By November several influential military officers had begun a movement to have the Junta relieve Carrera—no longer an active member of the Junta—of his military command. Juan Mackenna told O'Higgins that he was going to propose him to succeed Carrera. He even asked O'Higgins to try to influence Carrera to resign.[4] Not only was the campaign in the south lethargic and uninspired, but the army was in a miserable state. Mackenna observed that the troops could not mount an offensive; there was a shortage of money, food, and ammunition. Worse, no one had a suggestion of where or how to secure these necessities.

The Junta did not need much convincing. But before taking such a decisive step it solicited opinions from other government agencies. It is not surprising that the *cabildo* of Concepción supported Carrera instead of their own O'Higgins. It noted that soldiers follow their leaders, and these were the Carreras. O'Higgins was a fine person, it allowed, but the Carreras had the control and loyalty of the army.[5] The major fighting was taking place in Concepción, and the leading provincial *cabildo* was concerned exclusively with a military victory. The central Junta, on the other hand, was also concerned with Carrera's political powers. It relieved him and his two brothers of their military commands on November 27. The separation decree stated that the Carrera family had acquired so much military power that it governed the entire military force of Chile. Through such power, the Junta concluded, the members of the family were the "arbiters of the will of a million inhabitants." [6] On the same day the Junta named O'Higgins General-in-Chief of the army of restoration. He was informed of the appointment the following day. The Junta wanted immediate action. The new Chief was told that every moment lost in initiating active military operations amounted to a new evil.[7] It is interesting that though O'Higgins was now General-in-Chief of the army of restoration, he remained merely a colonel in the ordinary Chilean army. Such duality of rank was common during the era.

Before he heard of his appointment O'Higgins replied to a letter from the Junta seeking his opinion about the matter, stating that Carrera should not be replaced. He felt, much as did the *cabildo* of Concepción, that it would be deleterious to change leaders while the war was being fought.[8] And when he received the news he did not at once accept the new position. Rather, he proceeded to Concepción, and discussed with the *cabildo* the possibility of restoring Carrera to power. Word of O'Higgins' hesitancy created somber unrest in Talca. To the Junta's further embarrassment, an assembly of notables met in Santiago on December 4 and generously "applauded the wise resolutions that the Supreme Government of the State has taken." [9] O'Higgins received a letter early in December from Mackenna admonishing him to take command of the army and lead Chile to victory. Mackenna stated directly that if he did not assume command and the war was lost, he would be eternally responsible.[10] Though the letter was in Spanish it ended with the English words: "Courage; save, save your country." O'Higgins had great respect for Mackenna and no doubt was moved; he decided to travel to Talca to discuss the problem personally with the Junta. He left Concepción in the morning of December 6.

The trip took three days, part of which time was expended in eluding enemy troops. He arrived at Talca at three-thirty in the morning of December 9. An hour later he met with a hurriedly gathered Junta. Again he expressed the opinion that a change of generals would endanger the war effort. As a commander of guerrillas in a time of danger he had been successful, but he felt he lacked the necessary preparation to direct the entire war. In addition, though he was not without connections within the military, he believed that he did not enjoy the requisite prestige among officers to elicit order and subordination.[11] At midday he was sworn in as General-in-Chief.[12] We do not know what argument the Junta presented, but O'Higgins was generally susceptible to pleas of loyalty and patriotism. However, the Junta would have done well to listen to him: His self-evaluation was accurate.

The most important unknown element in all these political and military maneuvers was the manner in which Carrera would react. From Concepción, Carrera informed the Junta at Talca that he thoroughly agreed with the selection of O'Higgins as the officer to succeed him. But he did not recognize O'Higgins as General-in-Chief. While O'Higgins remained in Talca such a step might engender infinite disorder in his own troops. However, he would recognize O'Higgins as his superior once he arrived in Concepción. Since O'Higgins elected to remain in Talca, from which point he might better reconstruct his army, which was dispirited and in a dismal state both physically and mentally, his command of all forces was not recognized by the most important officer, Carrera. This did little to help general morale. O'Higgins' efforts at building a potent fighting force were frustrated by an even more conventional problem: the lack of financial resources. To heighten his anxiety, the enemy was faring well. Clarity is not served by referring to the invaders, as is usually done, as the royalists and the defenders as the patriots. Though the Peruvian-supported army was related directly to the Viceroy and the existing Spanish government, the defenders were also fighting in the name of Ferdinand. And, after all, a good many of those one is tempted to call the patriots were avowed royalists, opposed to any movement toward independence. Soldiers from Peru formed only the nucleus of the enemy army; most fighting men were recruited from Chile itself.

The interlopers presently were awaiting the arrival of fresh troops and supplies from Peru. It is true that Chile enjoyed the advantages of formidable natural barriers to foreign intrusion. On one flank was the cordillera, the Andes mountain range. To the north, the inhospitable desert; and to the south, the very opposite, a verdant territory rich in agricultural potential, but subject to so much rainfall and flooding each year that invading troops had to be supplied constantly from abroad. On the other flank was the ocean, which suggested that troops could be landed almost at will anywhere along the coast, but which, in the long run, meant that an army had to be supplied by sea exclusively. But under certain conditions these very factors worked in favor of the enemy. An invading army with an effective supply line to its homeland could remain in southern Chile for as long a time as it took the Chileans to conquer it. And this is the critical point: If the invaders were willing to take their time and secure the entire southern region, the Chileans would be forced to assume the offensive. The geography and climate of southern Chile decidedly favored a defensive movement. To compound matters in the present case, the Peruvians had not yet lost control of the large island of Chiloé, just off the southern tip of the Chilean mainland, which was employed as a staging area.

On the first day of 1814 a new force departed from Callao under the leadership of General Gabino Gaínza, who was ordered to take command of the Peruvian war effort in Chile. The party landed at Arauco, just south of Concepción, on January 31. But by this time the question of O'Higgins' authority was nearly answered. In the middle of January the Junta decided to send its own representative to Concepción with funds to pay the irritated troops. O'Higgins, who had stationed himself at Quirihue, north of Concepción, did not approve of the project. He feared that Carrera might interpret such a move as an infringement on his authority, and be provoked into disobedience. So tenuous was O'Higgins' command. However, when the Junta's representative arrived at Quirihue on his way to Concepción, O'Higgins greeted him respectfully and enjoined him to display the most circumspect moderation in his dealings with Carrera. But once he learned of the arrival of Gaínza, probably on the same day, O'Higgins decided to march into Concepción and personally take command of the war from that point. On February 1 the Junta wrote him indicating that speed was of great importance. The government wanted to impress upon him the urgency of taking Arauco. "Nothing is as prejudicial as delay: this is our ruin." [13] On the same day Carrera finally recognized O'Higgins as General-in-Chief. Having given up his position on the Junta in order to assume command of the war effort, and now having lost this, Carrera's official power was finally broken.

O'Higgins arrived in Concepción in the evening of February 2. To Mackenna he wrote the following day that the troops were in a sorry condition. Without proper clothing, food, and horses, the army appeared incapable of fighting. Without supplies the cause seemed lost. There were over two thousand soldiers in and around Concepción, all of whom were not impressed by their new leader. Many officers continued to expect their orders to come from Carrera, and at times he issued them. Though ostensibly friendly, Carrera mostly served to complicate the transition of command. But logistics remained the central problem. Mackenna wrote back from Quirihue that he did not doubt for a moment that O'Higgins' valorous troops, always invincible under his command, would overcome every obstacle placed in the way of the country's liberty. Considering that Mackenna more than any other individual was responsible for O'Higgins' receiving the command, these words of encouragement should not have cost him dearly. Yet his last words were an appropriate commentary on the state of the army. His own division, he told O'Higgins, was ready to march to the glories and dangers of war, but the nights already were long and cold, and the division urgently required additional tents.[14] O'Higgins complained to the central Junta of his own needs: ". . . we have arrived at the last extreme, surrounded by the enemy, without food, money, horses or clothing, all is lacking and nothing arrives. Thus, sir, there is nothing to do but make the final effort before we perish miserably."

The central Junta seemed more concerned about Carrera's disconcerting presence in Concepción than did O'Higgins. On February 12 it named Carrera Chilean Deputy to the government of the United Provinces of Río de la Plata. In telling O'Higgins of the appointment the Junta made it clear that whether Carrera accepted or not, he must leave Concepción within three days.[15] Carrera did not accept the proffered post, but neither did he leave Concepción. He told O'Higgins that he was planning to go to Santiago, but he made no effort to do so. It is not clear why O'Higgins disobeyed the Junta's orders. Even as Supreme Director he would manifest a distinct aversion to conflicts with other government officials. And he always displayed an intense loyalty to those whom he considered friends. It is probable that he simply did not want to ostracize Carrera by forcing him out of Concepción under such circumstances. All this further agonized the Junta. In the middle of February it elevated O'Higgins to the position of Governor-Intendant of the province of Concepción.[16] Now he was both military and political leader of the entire southern portion of the country. Still he did not order Carrera out of the actual war zone. The more power the Junta granted him the more it seemed to interfere with his administration. Toward the end of February it felt obliged to lecture him on the consequences of a military defeat. The loss of all or even the major part of his army would result in defeat for Chile as a whole. He was told not to enter into a general action in which victory was not a distinct probability, nor expose his forces in such a way that they might be encircled or exhausted by a superior enemy.[17]

While O'Higgins procrastinated in his responsibility toward Carrera, several influential civilian and military officials came to believe that Carrera's continued presence in Concepción was inimical to a successful prosecution of the war. On the first day of March a group of officers met in Concepción and drafted a note to O'Higgins calling for Carrera's expulsion from the city. That same evening O'Higgins wrote to Carrera asking him to leave Concepción. Carrera replied at once, saying that he would do so the following day.[18] Both of Carrera's brothers were ordered to leave also. José Miguel and Luis were captured by the Peruvian forces on their way north. On the day that O'Higgins made up his mind about Carrera, the central Junta left Talca for Santiago, their main task, the change of command having been completed.

The war, which was nearly a year old, now broke out of its ennui and developed a decisive momentum. The Junta arrived in Santiago on March 6. On March 12 it learned that Talca had fallen. Three days later the Senate promulgated a new basis of government. Because of the "critical circumstances of the day," the Junta was disbanded, and all executive powers were invested in a newly created Supreme Director. Except in the case of treaties of peace, declarations of war, new treaties of commerce, and public taxation, the Supreme Director would enjoy ample and unlimited powers and would not require senatorial approval for his decrees. His tenure was stipulated to be eighteen months. The Senate would be composed of seven members selected by him from a list of names presented by a junta of corporations.[19] Chile's first Supreme Director was thirty-seven-year-old Francisco de la Lastra, scion of one of the country's leading families. He had studied in Spain, where he became a naval officer, and resumed residence in Chile in 1803. After September 1810 he was charged by the patriots with the organization of naval forces. Though not possessed of brilliant abilities, Lastra was indeed competent.

O'Higgins learned of the disaster at Talca also on March 12.

His first concern was Santiago, that is, his rather difficult obligation of placing troops between Talca and the capital before the enemy chose to march farther north. Most of his two thousand troops began the march north that same day. Enemy marauders had intercepted many of the most important communiqués sent to and from O'Higgins in recent days, and he did not know exactly where Mackenna's troops were to the north. He remained in Concepción until March 14 in order to establish a government of sorts to function in his absence. By that day Mackenna anxiously awaited O'Higgins' arrival to lead the troops in the impending battle, and chided him for remaining in Concepción. But Mackenna also wanted the extra troops that his superior would bring. Gaínza's division was camped directly in front of him across the Itata River, and another division, under Lantaño, was on its way to join in an attack.[20]

To his permanent embarrassment, O'Higgins did not manage to unite his troops with those of Mackenna's until March 25. In his own defense he cited the inadequate means of transportation at his disposal and roads that were for a while impassable due to heavy rainfall. But he did arrive in the vicinity of the fighting before actually meeting Mackenna. On March 19, by his own account, he was attacked unsuccessfully by a small force. This he considered the first of two close Chilean victories. On the following day at four in the afternoon over a thousand of the enemy attacked Mackenna. As he observed to O'Higgins, the fighting was intense and lasted four hours. "Our loss has not been considerable, and that of the enemy horrible. . . ." It was the second victory in a row. Mackenna did not think that a new effort would be launched the next day, but requested that O'Higgins march closer so that the enemy could be caught in a cross fire.[21] Yet O'Higgins still did not move. With each day Mackenna believed the enemy was given the advantage of time. He had his back to Santiago and an enemy force in front of him: Under such circumstances he was unable to fathom O'Higgins' delay.

"Tell me in the name of God," Mackenna wrote to O'Higgins two days after his victory, "what has happened to you and your division." In these two days there was no enemy capable of obstructing their union. In the harshest terms he disparaged O'Higgins' dilatory practices, even challenging his valor: "You do not have to fear the enemy, because it is not in a state to attack you." What would they say in Santiago, he wanted to know, when they learn that we have been so near each other for two months, and when the country is in such imminent danger? "More activity, my dear friend; if not all is lost and this through your fault and lack of energy." [22] On the same day, perhaps after receiving Mackenna's disturbing message, O'Higgins wrote that though he felt there would be no further attack he would march immediately to join his force with Mackenna's. "I am going to march and I hope that you will tell me, as one experienced in this terrain, where I ought to situate myself." One cannot be sure, but he may have been using the want of such geographical knowledge as an excuse for not having marched earlier.[23]

By the end of March both the Chileans and Peruvians were marching north toward Santiago along parallel lines, often only a few miles apart. Gaínza reached Talca and there received supplies from the south. O'Higgins encamped at Quechereguas and prepared to defend the road to the capital. Though the Chilean army was superior in numbers to the enemy, many leading residents in Santiago were daily growing fearful that Gaínza might break out of Talca and capture the capital. Just at this time, while the two armies were holding each other to a standoff, Great Britain, acting under the assumption that it served her interests to stop the diversion of troops and gold from Spain, intervened. Captain Hillyar of the Royal Navy had been instructed to offer his good offices to the Peruvian and Chilean governments in an effort to secure a peace. Hillyar arrived in Santiago on April 16 and immediately informed Supreme Director Lastra of the conditions to a peace laid down by Viceroy Abascal. These were rejected at once. But within three days of Hillyar's arrival a treaty was drawn, and signed by Lastra.

By the Treaty of Lircay, as it came to be called in recognition of the river which separated the two armies, Chile acknowledged the sovereignty of Ferdinand VII and the authority of the Regency, and agreed to send a deputy to the Spanish *Cortes.* The Peruvian forces would evacuate the city of Talca within thirty hours of Gaínza's approval of the treaty, and the province of Concepción within a month. Commercial relations would be reestablished with the rest of the empire. Various sections treated of the exchange of prisoners and amnesty.[24] Gaínza met at Talca with O'Higgins and Mackenna to discuss any necessary modifications. O'Higgins had been elevated recently to the rank of brigadier so that the Chileans would have an officer at the field negotiations of equal rank with Brigadier Gaínza. The original document stated that O'Higgins would be the Chilean deputy to the *Cortes.* The soldiers decided that each side must exchange with the other three ranking officers to serve as hostages. They agreed that O'Higgins should be one of them, unless he would actually be called upon to represent Chile in Spain. The Senate later approved the three-man hostage system, but took O'Higgins' name out of the arrangement. The Senate also added to the treaty that O'Higgins would be the deputy to the *Cortes* only if elected to that position. Gaínza, O'Higgins, and Mackenna signed the treaty on May 3, 1814.[25]

But Gaínza began to question various points of the treaty the following day. On the fifth O'Higgins wrote his counterpart that he was dismayed by this lack of good faith. Two days later Gaínza was informed that the government in Santiago had ratified the treaty. Both sides began complying with its requirements. However, it was not a generally popular treaty. Gaínza commanded only about a thousand troops in Talca and probably would have been defeated somewhere along the march to Santiago. On the other hand, his supporters were scandalized by his decision to evacuate and subject them to the vengeance of the Chilean army. Since Gaínza had not been authorized by the Viceroy to sue for peace, it is likely that he was playing for time in which to organize his forces under the assumption that the treaty would not be approved in Lima. These same factors may well have influenced Lastra. He, too, probably wanted time, and in his case, distance. He was doubtless hesitant to gamble the future of all of Chile on one battle which might owe its outcome to O'Higgins' military competence. The Supreme Director probably hoped—especially since many compatriots believed the advantage was theirs—that the treaty would be rejected in Lima; but once the enemy had retreated back into Concepción. Talca was just too close.[26]

Gaínza did not fully appreciate the animosity generated by the treaty in the south until he reached Chillán on May 18. Consequently, he initiated a program of delay and found many excuses for slowing down the departure. While both sides were avoiding a final decision about the matter, a fortuitous event occurred. On May 12 José Miguel Carrera and his brother Luis escaped from Chillán and made their way north. They may have acted prematurely, since Gaínza was planning to release them anyway. O'Higgins greeted Carrera affectionately when he reached Talca. In fact, the brothers spent the first night in O'Higgins' own house. This surprised not a few people, who understood that Carrera's presence at a time when there was considerable antigovernment sentiment over the Treaty of Lircay might produce domestic disorder. Several officers asked Carrera to stay out of public sight. It appears that O'Higgins made a similar request. On the sixteenth, two days after arriving in Talca, the Carreras rode north to their father's hacienda, situated to the southwest of Santiago. They planned not to enter the capital. Supreme Director Lastra was thoroughly shocked to learn that O'Higgins had permitted the Carreras to take the road to Santiago. Not only did he reprimand the General-in-Chief, but he made it perfectly clear that the civilian government gave the orders. "Henceforth it is necessary that Your Excellency," the Director told the General, "abandoning that attitude of kindness that is characteristic of you, firmly support the decisions of government. . . ." [27]

All through the month of June Gaínza did little to comply with his part of the bargain, and the Chileans did even less to force the issue. Approximately three months after the treaty had been signed, O'Higgins, still stationed in Talca, decided to send two emissaries to Chillán to encourage Gaínza to observe the treaty. Lastra approved, and Isidro Pineda and Miguel Zañartu were sent south. O'Higgins appreciated that Gaínza felt obliged to wait for word on the treaty from Lima before leaving Chile entirely, but he thought that the Peruvians could at least concentrate their forces at Concepción and Talcahuano in an act of good faith. Gaínza showed himself to be more ingenious as a diplomat than he had been as a soldier. He held off the Chilean delegates by such maneuvers as refusing to accept their credentials. Once their patience was worn thin they returned to Talca, declaring their mission a failure. O'Higgins agreed, and on July 26 asked the Supreme Director to declare a state of war. With the proper supplies he was sure he could lead the country to victory.

Though O'Higgins could not have guessed it, his timing was awkward. Three days earlier José Miguel Carrera successfully carried off another *coup* and established himself as the head of government. Lastra, Mackenna, and several other important officials were thrown into jail. On July 25 he announced that the new government would recognize the Treaty of Lircay. O'Higgins was ordered to remain in command of the armed forces. Word of these events and decisions did not reach Talca until after O'Higgins sent his request for war to Lastra. Carrera's personal representative did not arrive in Talca until the twenty-eighth. He was soon arrested. On the same day O'Higgins convoked a Council of War of all officers in the vicinity with the rank of captain or higher. Forty officers met and elected not to recognize the new Junta in Santiago. All those present signed the statement. Among them were Ramón Freire and Joaquín Prieto, two future presidents of Chile. O'Higgins decided that on the following day he would form his own junta.[28]

A junta was not created in Talca the next day. Instead, the Council of War met again and decided to send troops to Santiago at once.[29] A *cabildo abierto* in Talca the same day decided not to recognize the Santiago Junta.[30] However, O'Higgins thought he might be able to achieve the desired results without sending troops and chancing open war between Chileans. Especially when an enemy army continued to occupy a considerable amount of real estate in the realm. Instead of troops, he sent copies of the statements drawn by the Council and the *cabildo*. In a private letter to Carrera—according to Barros Arana—he suggested that peace could be maintained if the new regime discontinued its persecutions, its exiles and imprisonments; and called a congress to choose a permanent government.[31] These notes arrived in Santiago on August 1. Carrera characteristically avoided a direct answer; rather, he placated O'Higgins with banalities about patriotism and friendship. And the persecutions continued. On August 7 O'Higgins sent part of his army in the direction of the capital. He departed with another division five days later. About fifteen hundred soldiers constituted the total force. Joaquín Prieto remained in Talca in command of another six hundred soldiers.

Leading the vanguard of his army, about three hundred men, O'Higgins crossed the strategic Maipo River, situated just to the south of Santiago. Ahead of him was the main body of Carrera's army. Yet O'Higgins took so little precaution that it seems he expected no resistance. This is surprising, given the proximity of the Maipo to Santiago, the last geographical barrier on the route from the south. Not only did O'Higgins cut himself off from his main force, but his poorly equipped troops, enormously outnumbered in manpower, munitions, and artillery, had at their back a river that could be forded but not easily during the August rain season. Yet he marched his troops into battle. Strangely, they were successful in the initial contact. Captain Freire displayed an ability to lead a small band of cavalry that would be decisive in many another battle. But this early good fortune served to draw O'Higgins closer to Carrera's entrenched positions and artillery. The main battle commenced about four o'clock in the afternoon with the artillery firing continuously for nearly an hour. O'Higgins' horse was shot out from under him. His troops suffered many casualties. Once the attackers began their disorderly retreat, Carrera ordered in his reserves to assume the offensive and charge their flank. Though O'Higgins lost only twenty dead, many more were wounded or taken prisoner; among the latter were four officers.

O'Higgins crossed the Maipo with about a hundred of his soldiers and proceeded to rendezvous with the remainder. He sent orders south instructing the main body of the army to join him immediately. He hoped to cross the Maipo again in two days. It is quite impossible to perceive what motivated him to such precipitate action and unsound military tactics. Even with reinforcements he planned to march right through Carrera's army rather than outflank it and attempt to reach Santiago first. It was precisely at this juncture that both armies received news that altered their battle plans.

In June Viceroy Abascal disapproved the Treaty of Lircay and mounted a new expedition against Chile. Gaínza informed the Viceroy that he held most of the province of Concepción, including the key urban centers, and commanded nearly twenty-five hundred disciplined troops, not counting the local militia bodies that could be mustered into service. Abascal chose Mariano Osorio to lead the expedition and take charge of the army in Chile. Osorio was born in Seville to a famous family, studied at the prestigious Segovia school of artillery, and was sent in 1812 to Lima as a colonel in charge of all artillery units. He was also assigned to be Professor of Mathematics in Lima's military school. A fleet carrying six hundred soldiers and war materiel sailed from Callao on July 19 and arrived at the port of Talcahuano on August 13. Five days later Osorio was in Chillán, and there accepted Gaínza's resignation. On August 20, Osorio prepared a note "to those who command in Chile," perhaps in recognition of the uncertainty of that fact, announcing that the Viceroy did not approve the treaty, which was contrary to the honor of Spain and Gaínza's orders. All Chileans were given exactly ten days in which to throw down their arms and swear allegiance to the King and his representatives—which meant the Viceroy. At the termination of that period hostilities would be renewed, and the responsibility for further bloodshed would devolve upon the Chileans. A generous amnesty awaited all soldiers—especially officers—who complied with these conditions, but those who did not would be responsible to God.

Osorio dispatched an agent, Captain Pasquel, to carry his message to Santiago on Sunday, August 21. He arrived at O'Higgins' encampment, several miles south of the Maipo, and conferred about the demands. O'Higgins felt that only the government in

Santiago—which he supposedly did not recognize—could act on such a pregnant matter. He therefore cleared the way for Pasquel to ride on to the capital. But he also sent his own representative to Santiago to inform the government that this was not the time for internal strife, rather, all Chilean troops should be united. This in light of the fact that it was he who created the strife and the division in forces. The Junta received Osorio's message still on the same day and immediately jailed its bearer. Just coincident with these events was the arrival in Santiago of news that on May 2, 1814, Ferdinand VII, in Valencia, had dissolved the *Cortes*, repealed the notably liberal Constitution of Cádiz, and proclaimed the restoration of absolutism. The Chilean government no longer could justify theoretically its position against the Viceroy of Peru. But the inherent paradox does not seem to have bothered anyone.

A day after it read Osorio's demands, the four-man Junta, one of whom was Carrera, decreed that they were not acceptable. Thus, though the Junta said exactly what it was not going to do, it did not indicate what it was going to do. On the last day of the month O'Higgins wrote to Carrera that a general assembly should be called to create a new government. No member of Carrera's or his own army should be allowed to be a delegate to the assembly. O'Higgins said he would turn over command of his troops to whomever the new government selected. Carrera, as he had been in the past and would be several more times in the future, was bewildered by O'Higgins' naïveté. The President of the Junta, whose army was victorious and had been increased in size in recent days, whose control over the capital was secure, was being asked to relinquish his position and contribute to the creation of a new government which might or might not include him. In his *Diario Militar* Carrera wrote: "One cannot arrive at greater stupidity than that of the general (O'Higgins)." It was the type of thing, Carrera thought, that only O'Higgins could propose.[32] In this, Carrera was more accurate than not. Much to the chagrin of both his political allies and foes, this would be true of him also as Supreme Director.

Rather than express his demeaning views to O'Higgins, Carrera merely made some general statements about the proposal and suggested that the two confer about the matter. In the morning of September 2, 1814, the two generals, each with an aide, met at a hacienda near the Maipo. No record of the talks was kept. Near evening O'Higgins departed, saying that he would give his decision on the talks within twenty-four hours. The following evening he rode into Santiago and announced to Carrera that he recognized the present government. On the fourth the two issued a joint statement urging the public to support the government in the forthcoming confrontation with the invaders. The public was informed that the army of the capital and the army of restoration of the south were united. Whether they realized it or not, the generals closed with a statement of principles. They were going to fight "to avenge the country and secure its security, its liberty, its prosperity with the sublime triumph of *union.*" [33] But security and liberty from what? Ferdinand was back on the throne of Spain and Chile had not declared its independence. Though this step was not taken officially until 1818, it seems fair to suggest that the Manifesto of September 4 made it clear that Chile in fact had unofficially declared its independence. Yet Carrera and O'Higgins certainly were not authorized to speak for all Chileans, not even for all residents of the territory they controlled. The 1818 declaration of independence was really *de facto* recognition of an attitude that evolved slowly between September 1810 and September 1814. Suffice to say that Chileans were told on September 4 that they were about to fight for their independence, if not from what.

The news was made public just in time: The following day Osorio reached the banks of the Maule River, just south of Talca, received the Junta's refusal of his demands, and announced to his troops that the war was now resumed. In Chillán he had organized a fairly well-armed and equipped force of about five thousand troops. Most important, however, was that included among them were several contingents of highly trained and experienced professionals from Peru and Spain. On August 28 Osorio had ordered part of his army north. The rest followed during the next three days. On the twenty-ninth the vanguard took Talca, which had been left defenseless.

On September 9 the Junta granted Carrera the power to proceed as he saw fit to insure victory. But Carrera did not have a definite plan of action, and the vagaries of his consequent indecision vexed O'Higgins, who commanded the first line of defense. O'Higgins desired to establish a defense just to the south of the town of Rancagua, situated on the road between Santiago and Talca. He considered Talca the most appropriate place to make a stand should the outer line fall. To Carrera he wrote on September 14 that in Rancagua one could conduct a vigorous defense without involving too many troops in the action. The Chilean army in retreat could make a stand in Rancagua and still save the country, but steps would have to be taken immediately to prepare the town for such a holding action. O'Higgins came to this conclusion while stationed in Maipú, a short distance from the capital. On September 16 he informed Carrera that the army was generally in good shape and would march to Rancagua on the following day. However, the artillery units were very discontented because they were improperly clothed, were not permitted leave to visit Santiago, and were owed money. In fact, the entire army lacked supplies and experienced officers. As it turned out, O'Higgins was conservative in his estimation of discontent.

The army did not march on the seventeenth as planned. The night before, the entire body of artillerymen attempted to desert. The exodus was stopped by an imaginative officer who promised the arrival of proper uniforms on the morrow. "I note," O'Higgins observed calmly to Carrera, "in the soldiers, principally in those, a general discontent, and in order to avoid a fatal result it seems to me desirable that artillerymen from the capital come to relieve them." This was written after the attempted desertion. It is not certain that these new troops arrived by the eighteenth, but on that day O'Higgins marched his division of about a thousand men toward Rancagua. As he prepared to leave Maipú O'Higgins stated his confidence in Rancagua once again to Carrera: "This spot certainly is impregnable if it is cared for as it should be." He requested among other things a thousand additional infantrymen, three hundred cavalrymen armed with rifles, and an equal number of lancers. With such additional force he would be responsible for keeping the enemy at bay. But if the defense depended on the force he had on hand at present, "things were not so sure." But there was no meeting of the minds here. While O'Higgins seems to have placed trust in his superior, the reverse was not at all true. In fact, Carrera believed that O'Higgins wanted the additional troops not to fight the enemy but to control the recent deserters. Writing later in his *Diario,* Carrera noted that O'Higgins' "obstinacy and his desire for vengeance equalled his ambition." [34] This speaks volumes for an understanding of the impending disaster.

O'Higgins reached Rancagua on September 20 and immediately began constructing its defenses. Scouting parties reported that the enemy was encamped at the Cachapoal River, a short distance from the town. At two in the afternoon he wrote to Carrera that he was preparing "to defend this place at all costs down to the last man." In another letter written the same day, he reported that he had only twenty thousand rounds of ammunition, not all of which were likely to fire. It was not enough to stage a lengthy defense. He asked Carrera to send ten thousand additional rounds right away. On the same day Carrera wrote that he should not engage the enemy in a general action until the other Chilean divisions arrived. If making his defense at Rancagua was not a distinct advantage under future military conditions, O'Higgins should retreat toward the capital.[35] O'Higgins replied on the twenty-first that he had learned that two thousand men would join him momentarily. "If these forces arrive here before the enemy advances with their main body, it seems that we will defend this spot with full security." Again he pleaded the case for a defense at Rancagua, but added that if the circumstances were unfavorable he would pull back. The following day he reported that nothing novel had occurred. "If the enemy does not advance with all its army within two days, we can say that we will be impenetrable in this place, and consequently the defense of the realm assured."

But O'Higgins had more than just war to worry about. His mother and sister were in Santiago freed from their captivity but destitute of their basic necessities. On September 22, with the enemy ready to attack, O'Higgins asked Carrera to order the treasury to give his mother the eight months of salary owed him by the government. But only if this would not aggrieve the public treasury. Two days later he wrote Carrera that when he made the request he did not know that the government already had given his mother a thousand pesos and a house in which to live. In thanks he made a gift of the four thousand pesos owed him by the treasury to the government, and noted that to this sum he was adding the thousand advanced to his mother. A sum, he acknowledged, he could not pay just then, but which he would pay when possible.

Osorio did not attack as soon as O'Higgins had expected, thus allowing the Chileans more time to devote to perfecting their defenses. Carrera ordered him to take extreme care with the gunpowder. And with practiced equanimity O'Higgins replied that he was doing just that. The lack of proper clothing continued to undermine morale, and he requested additional uniforms. But the financial resources of the government were such that Carrera could not purchase clothing. In fact, he announced a mandatory discount on military salaries. O'Higgins wrote immediately that such a step was hardly desirable while the troops were awaiting battle: Carrera agreed and rescinded the decree.

Once O'Higgins had recognized Carrera's Junta he no longer

was General-in-Chief of Chile's main army. The structure of the army was altered, and Carrera became General-in-Chief of the Chilean army, with O'Higgins a general in charge of one division, the southern vanguard. So little confidence did Carrera have in O'Higgins that he did not even allow him command of the over-all defense of the south. Though one cannot be sure of the exact figures, it appears that O'Higgins' division comprised nearly twelve hundred men and six cannons. A second division, of about nineteen hundred men, was sent from the capital under the command of Juan José Carrera. And a third division, of about nine hundred men, was sent under the command of Luis Carrera. In addition, Luis was made commander of artillery. By September 29, both nepotist divisions had taken up their positions. Juan José stationed his troops to the east of Rancagua and Luis to the north. With such reinforcements O'Higgins would not have to concentrate too much on the advisability of a retreat toward the capital once a general engagement commenced.

But it seems that O'Higgins expected the two divisions to join him directly in Rancagua. "If we manage to unite the entire force at this point," he wrote to Carrera, "not only will we make ourselves impenetrable, but also we will be able to give some bad times to the pirate Osorio, and his gang of murderers." However, Carrera was not eager for both military and political reasons, no doubt, to place the total southern force under the command of O'Higgins. He himself left Santiago on September 30 to take charge of the whole operation. Only about three hundred troops remained in the capital. Others had been sent to Valparaíso and intermediate points to protect the flank against a possible sea invasion. The army that Carrera was going to meet was smaller in number than the Peruvian forces, not as well equipped, not as disciplined, and not as well commanded.

On the same day that Carrera headed south, a messenger from Osorio rode into Rancagua with a note to be delivered to his counterpart. O'Higgins immediately forwarded it north. The Viceroy had sent new instructions to Osorio that had only recently reached him. Osorio was informed that conditions were so precarious in Peru that if he had not yet brought the war in Chile to a conclusion he should attempt to make the best peace arrangement possible and embark with the major part of his army immediately for Peru. While Osorio was disposed to comply with the Viceroy's orders, many of his subordinates preferred to continue toward what they considered certain victory. He came around to their point of view, but to simulate compliance with the orders he sent a new offer of peace to Santiago, which he assumed at any rate might serve to split the Chilean camp.

On the same day that his agent reached Rancagua, Osorio mobilized his entire army and by dawn of October 1 had moved it across the Cachapoal. O'Higgins at once moved out of Rancagua with some troops to test the enemy, but he soon learned that Juan José's division had occupied the town, so he returned. Actually, Carrera's division was in disorderly retreat. In the confusion most of the cavalry found the road to Santiago and headed for the capital. This is probably the first point of dispute in an event noted for its historical controversy. Some say that the potential use of the cavalry was lost because O'Higgins refused it entrance into the town. It has not been demonstrated that this was the case. Certainly, mounted soldiers had no place in O'Higgins' plan of defense, the main point of which was the central plaza, which had four entrances. Here trenches were dug. Some soldiers were stationed outside the plaza, but only to slow down the attack. Several hundred additional cavalrymen would find no place in such entrenched warfare. But, it must be noted, they could have been used by the third division. But, again, we do not know exactly what prompted the cavalry's flight past Rancagua.

Now with two divisions and two brigadiers in Rancagua there existed a question of command. Theoretically the older brigadier, in this case Juan José Carrera, was entitled to the command, but he wisely deferred to O'Higgins, perhaps in consequence of the loss of prestige he had suffered during the 1813 campaigns. Once his leadership was recognized, O'Higgins began taking the final defense precautions. From the town's highest church tower he saw the enemy advancing on all fronts. Thus, he placed two cannons at each of the four entrances to the plaza. In the various towers and homes near the plaza he placed marksmen. At the trenches and in the tower of the Church of the Merced flew the national flag to which the soldiers had attached black cloth to indicate that they would not capitulate.

By ten in the morning Osorio had deployed his troops and anticipated an early victory. But each attack was repulsed. The fighting continued all through the day, and by nightfall Osorio was struck with the full implication of his decision to disobey the Viceroy's orders. The Chileans believed that they had taken the day, and the Peruvians were inclined to agree until they learned, probably from deserters, of the great number of casualties and the shortage of munitions within the central plaza. As Osorio prepared to continue the fight he ordered the entire flow of water into the plaza cut off. Once a second day of assault seemed unavoidable, O'Higgins manifested a fearful concern over the whereabouts of the third division and Carrera himself. At nine in the evening he sent a messenger to seek out Carrera with this laconic note: "If munitions come and the third division charges, all is done." [36] Carrera was positioned just to the north of Rancagua. After reading the note he replied that munitions would have to be sent in at the point of bayonets. "Tomorrow at dawn," he announced to O'Higgins, "this division will make its sacrifice." As it turned out, it was an empty promise, but one which rallied the troops in the town.

Quite enough erratic shooting occurred during the night to allow the exhausted troops little or no sleep. Nor had they eaten during the day. But once the messenger returned bearing Carrera's promise, a feeling of optimism suffused the plaza. At dawn of October 2, O'Higgins climbed the tower of the Church of the Merced and anxiously awaited the sight of the distant dust which would announce the arrival of the third division and the General-in-Chief. As the sun rose Osorio renewed the attack. Disconcerted by the stubborn resistance, he could not decide whether to continue or retreat. Several of his officers convinced him to divert the expected reinforcements. At about eleven o'clock O'Higgins saw the approaching third division and spread the word to his troops. This was enough to sustain them in their effort. But not only was the third division tardy, it met determined and unexpected resistance from the Peruvians. From this point exactly what we know of the battle is subject to much personal interpretation on the part of the participants. Once he knew Carrera was at the outskirts of the town, O'Higgins mustered his cavalry and prepared to attack from the plaza. Within an hour Carrera and the third division were routed and in flight. Carrera later stated that he had not pursued the charge since he thought his compatriots had capitulated or were in the process of so doing.

In spite of the dolorous departure of the third division the plaza continued to hold. In part, this was due to a simple desire to survive; in part, it was due to the febrile efforts of O'Higgins, who moved among the trenches under fire to encourage the troops. By midday of the second his men had been fighting for about thirty hours. Not only were they without water for themselves, but equally important there was no water for the cannons, and now they were beginning to explode. Then a part of the ammunition supply caught fire and blew up. By three in the afternoon the battle was nearly over. O'Higgins formed a column of about five hundred mounted horsemen and prepared to charge through the enemy. That is, anyone who could get a horse was invited along. The column jumped over Chilean and Peruvian trenches and ran right through a surprised enemy cavalry outfit to safety. Probably about a fifth of the column was lost through death or capture. But by then the enemy had taken the plaza and commenced inflicting horrendous penalties upon the stubborn defenders.[37]

It was a military defeat of major proportions. The Chileans started their defense with about seventeen hundred men. They lost about six hundred dead, three hundred wounded, and another four hundred taken prisoner. The enemy suffered fewer dead and wounded. The path to Santiago was relatively open. The key to a Chilean victory would have been the arrival of Carrera with men and supplies. So many varying and heartily conflicting accounts of the battle exist that it is not likely that we shall ever know precisely why Carrera did not continue into the plaza.[38] The truth has long ago been lost in the vortex of historical debate.

Yet in a certain sense Rancagua represented a victory for the Chileans. O'Higgins became—especially in later years—the hero of the independence movement. The Chileans even in defeat had made a tenacious and heroic stand in defense of their country. Between October 1814 and February 1817, when the reconquest of Chile was consummated, Chileans in exile had ample time to elevate Rancagua into a battle that could inspire the hearts of young and old alike.

While Rancagua was being defended, the population of Santiago suffered agonizing trepidation. Even before the battle was decided, plans were formulated to evacuate the city. Carrera reached the capital before dawn on October 3 and soon ordered the city abandoned. O'Higgins arrived at about eight o'clock and attempted to convince him that all was not lost, that the capital could yet be defended. But Carrera demurred. This was the last meeting ever held between the two leaders. By evening of October 4, 1814, a long, uneven line of émigrés stretched toward the town of Los Andes, situated at the foot of the Andes along the route to Mendoza. Carrera left on the fourth, as did O'Higgins with his family. Osorio entered the undefended capital late in the afternoon of the sixth.

Thus came to an end the *Patria Vieja,* the period in Chilean history that stretches from September 18, 1810 to the defeat at Rancagua.

CHAPTER IV

The Reconquest

OVER THREE THOUSAND PEOPLE GATHERED AT LOS ANDES WITH THE improbable intention of crossing the Andes in October 1814, when the snows had not yet melted. For such a number there was too little food, too little shelter, and too few pack animals. To their lasting credit, the soldiers helped the civilians in every way possible. By October 9 news of the disaster had reached Mendoza, and Governor José de San Martín of the province of Cuyo began sending supplies and animals back across the mountains to the Chileans. Probably the knowledge that the enemy was closing in at their backs spurred the marchers on. At any rate, they made it to Mendoza, and from there to other parts of the United Provinces of Río de la Plata.

O'Higgins, with his mother and sister, spent much of the remainder of 1814 and 1815 in Buenos Aires. Like many another Chilean exile he had two central concerns. One was providing the basic necessities of life for himself and his family. At times, this was indeed an exasperating task, requiring that the family periodically modify its standard of living. The other was the creation of a plan to liberate the homeland. It was probably this that kept him occupied most, this that furnished his *raison d'être*. Eventually he conceived of an ambitious plan that called for an invading force of at least six thousand men. They would form four divisions. Three would attack by land and the fourth by sea around the Cape. But the main concern of the officials in Buenos Aires was not the possibility of mounting an invasion to Chile, but, rather, the possibility that an invasion was going to come from Chile.

When at the end of May 1815 the government in Buenos Aires feared that an expected major expedition from Spain under General Morillo would choose the Río de la Plata region as its point of invasion, O'Higgins offered his services as a soldier for the proposed defense. The government was inclined to accept the offer, but the need was removed when it was learned that Morillo had landed in Venezuela. However, in January 1816 rumor had it that an invasion was being prepared on the Chilean side of the Andes. O'Higgins was asked by the government to proceed to the city of Mendoza to take part in the defense of the country. To facilitate the trip the government granted him five hundred pesos as expense money.[1] He arrived in Mendoza along with his mother and sister on February 21. Such was his penury that he had to sell his carriage for spending money.

It was here that he came into contact with José de San Martín, the man who would engineer the liberation of Chile. Born in the Viceroyalty of La Plata and educated as a soldier in Spain, San Martín arrived in Buenos Aires after the independence movement began, but in time to take an active part in the organization of the military. He left the army for the governorship of Cuyo under the pretext of poor health, but it is quite likely that he believed his continental plan better could be brought to fruition from Cuyo, a province which bordered on and included part of the Andes, than from Buenos Aires. The permanent independence of the United Provinces, San Martín was convinced, could be insured only by the liberation of the rest of the continent. This meant that the powerful and prestigious Viceroyalty of Peru must be liberated sooner or later. There were several ways of approaching Peru, but San Martín came to believe that it would be best to secure the freedom of Chile first.

Once he arrived in Mendoza, O'Higgins was confronted by two especially distressing problems. One was the nature of his relationship to the Argentine army, for he was after all a Chilean brigadier; and the other was the need to obtain enough money on which to live. The first was resolved within a week of his arrival. He was recognized as an Argentine brigadier and permitted an official guard, but allowed no salary. In March he had to ask San Martín to order the treasury to give him one hundred pesos. San Martín had already requested a ruling on the matter of O'Higgins' finances earlier. The Secretary of War informed him that O'Higgins should be given the salary of a colonel of infantry when actually in service and one half that sum when not in service. At the end of the month San Martín ordered the start of payment.[2]

Right from the outset, San Martín treated O'Higgins with the utmost respect and took especial pains to secure his position in the foreign army. Even before O'Higgins reached Mendoza, San Martín knew that no invasion from Chile was in the offing. Thus he decided to travel to Buenos Aires for talks with government officials. In his absence he requested the Interim Director, Ignacio

Alvarez, to rule that the political and military command of Cuyo be delegated to the oldest officer present in the province. But before an answer to his request was received, O'Higgins arrived. The situation was now markedly different, and San Martín urged Alvarez to allow him to delegate political authority to the *cabildo* of Mendoza and military command to O'Higgins. The answer from Buenos Aires was that military command must be placed in an Argentine officer. Embarrassment was averted when San Martín canceled his trip. The posture assumed by the government may well have been inspired by the influence of Carrera and his followers in Buenos Aires. Carrera had his own plans for the liberation of Chile and was actively engaged in the winning of converts.

The question of provisional authority came up again in June when San Martín decided to travel to Córdoba for an official conference. On June 17 he appointed O'Higgins president of the permanent military commission in Mendoza, a position of influence and prestige. On the following day he granted him military command of the province for the month of his proposed absence. Political authority went to the *cabildo* of Mendoza.[3] While San Martín had great confidence in O'Higgins, he no doubt had considered the benign effect of such a gesture on the Chilean military community in Mendoza, now a central feature in his continental plan.

O'Higgins' tenure as military commander was short-lived and rather routine. He kept a diary for the period of July 3 to the end of the month, when San Martín returned. The entries are few and sparse; there is no indication that anything unusual occurred during the month.[4] By August he was immersed in the final plans for the invasion of Chile. On July 21 he wrote a friend in Buenos Aires that the expedition to Chile was now a sure thing. At the same time he asked that any available French books on military tactics be sent him, the more modern the better. And as he thought of it, any books dealing with the art of war would be welcome, so long as they also be relatively recent. This probably was not an unfamiliar predicament for many of the era's patriot-soldiers: On the one hand, he was preparing for a major war; on the other, he was concerned with his inadequacy as a militarist.

During the last months of 1816, San Martín reviewed intelligence reports, listened to the advice of his subordinates, and came to a final decision about the nature of the operation. O'Higgins continued to sponsor a combined land-sea invasion. A small division would be sent around the Cape by ship. Its task would be to blockade the chief ports, including Valparaíso. Another small division would enter Chile by land through the northern province of Coquimbo. Here, O'Higgins assured San Martín, the local militia would rise up and join it. The main body of the army would attack over the Andes directly. The plan required the quick liberation of the south. O'Higgins believed that the province of Concepción should be secured before a serious attack on Santiago be initiated. Concepción was more warlike than Santiago, he observed, and had more than eight thousand cavalry militia. He no doubt thought that these could be won over. And in Concepción, he added almost as an appropriate epitaph to three centuries of Chilean history, there were "more than six thousand Indians who are aficionados of war." Control of Concepción would inhibit a retreat from Santiago, but if the invasion force took Santiago first, the defenders could return to the south and continue to prosecute the war from that ideal position.[5] And how well O'Higgins knew this to be true! In its complication and reliance upon perfect timing, it was a bold plan. But it was precisely for this reason that San Martín rejected it in favor of his own plan, which was less speculative and more militarily sound. The invasion would be entirely by land, but diversionary actions were included. The Argentine elected to concentrate his invasion on Chile's central region first.

San Martín mobilized the Army of the Andes on January 9, 1817. On the thirteenth a force of eighty soldiers and twenty cavalrymen, under the command of Lieutenant Colonel Ramón Freire, headed over one of the southern passes. Its destination was southern Chile and its purpose was to create a guerrilla diversion. Colonel Juan Gregorio de las Heras, who had commanded an Argentine auxiliary force in Chile during the 1813–14 campaigns, led a large division toward the famous Uspallata Pass on the eighteenth. On the twentieth another division headed for a third pass. The main body of the army was made up of two additional divisions, one of which was commanded by O'Higgins, with the other commanded by Argentine General Soler. O'Higgins marched his division toward the *Garganta de los Patos*—the Ravine of the Ducks—on the twenty-first. The rest of the army followed their authorized routes within a matter of days. On the twenty-fourth San Martín began the ascent with his official suite.

Since it was now clear that one side was defending Chile in the name of the restored King and his imperial structure, and one was invading so that Chileans could have a free choice concerning their relationship with the King and the empire, one can properly refer to them as the royalists and the patriots. With some justification the royalists did not expect an entire army of several thousand men to climb over the Andes, even during the southern summer, and cut through the Chilean flank, the central region leading directly to Santiago. It was more than merely a daring feat, the moving of an army over passes thousands of feet higher than the St. Bernard Pass in the Alps, with the vertiginous heights and rarefied atmosphere constantly taking their toll. It was also a severe challenge to San Martín's abilities at logistics. The troops had to carry all their war materiel with them. Food, ammunition, weapons, artillery, all had to be carried over mountains and across ravines. But this was precisely San Martín's forte: He could organize an army and move it from one point to another better than any other militarist on the southern half of the continent. His achievement now ranks as one of the world's most impressive military successes. It has not gone unremarked in history.

On February 4, 1817, the advanced guard made its first contact with the enemy, and by the seventh easily controlled several strategic points. By the eighth it controlled the Valley of Aconcagua. The patriots and royalists chose the plains of Chacabuco, to the northeast of the capital, to decide the issue. O'Higgins' division comprised about eight hundred and fifty soldiers and another hundred porters. Along with Soler's division of somewhat larger size, it would form the main fighting unit. The royalist army comprised about eighteen hundred troops, a force so small that one can be sure that Governor Marcó del Pont did not expect the invasion from the Andes, or did not anticipate San Martín's genius for transporting so many men.

The Battle of Chacabuco was fought on February 12, 1817. According to the battle plans the patriots were to conduct a two-phased attack. O'Higgins would fake an attack at the enemy's flank, throwing him off guard, and Soler, with a larger division, would make the main charge and rout the defenders. But rather than just feigning an attack, once O'Higgins got near the enemy he did in fact attack. By the time Soler could bring up his division the battle had unexpectedly ended. By the book, it was certainly a military error on O'Higgins's part. He later claimed that San Martín learned immediately of the engagement and ordered Soler to move up his troops for support.[6] It was typical of O'Higgins to manifest little restraint under battle, to think with almost irrational consistency that victory was always there for the taking. And, interestingly, San Martín was just the opposite: He moved slowly and carefully; to his subordinates, sometimes lethargically.

O'Higgins asked Soler to pursue the fleeing enemy at once and intercept Marcó before he could reach Valparaíso with the treasury. Soler was not at the moment ready to agree with his colleague on anything. San Martín arrived at the battle scene shortly, and O'Higgins repeated his plea. But he also refused, in the hope of securing the victory by keeping his army together.

Chilean historians have generally recognized O'Higgins' tactical mistake, but they have also given him credit for the victory. What is most important is that San Martín did not contribute to a split within the ranks. In his report to Buenos Aires written the day of the battle, he only praised both O'Higgins and Soler, speaking of their "brilliant conduct, valor and skills. . . ." No mention was made of any aberration in battle plans. He also noted that the enemy suffered four hundred and fifty dead, and six hundred taken prisoner, among them thirty officers. He added that his own army lost less than a hundred men.[7] Two days later he notified the new Governor of Cuyo, somewhat prematurely: "All Chile is already ours." His army had entered Santiago, and Marcó was in flight. Marcó had fled to Valparaíso, but could not find a ship there ready to sail, so he headed south, and San Martín's soldiers presently were attempting to overtake him.[8] Once he realized that the royalists would offer no resistance in the central region, San Martín had dispatched troops to capture Marcó. And at this they were successful.

As soon as the royalists fled Santiago the *cabildo* elected Francisco Ruiz Tagle Interim Governor. On February 15 an assembly of notables elected San Martín Governor of Chile and granted him unlimited powers. San Martín, in a note to Ruiz Tagle, refused the position. On the following day the assembly again elected San Martín, and again he refused. It then proceeded at the same session to elect O'Higgins Interim Supreme Director.[9] O'Higgins was San Martín's choice and the choice of the government that had sponsored the liberation of Chile. That O'Higgins would become Supreme Director had been decided long before in Buenos Aires; San Martín's instructions were specific on the matter. O'Higgins himself knew of this decision before crossing the Andes.[10]

But this is exactly as it should have been. It was natural for the Chileans to express their gratitude to San Martín, the man who quite spectacularly liberated them. And it was natural for the Argentines to want O'Higgins as head of the new government. Chile, after all, represented merely the first stage in the Argentine plan for the liberation of the South American continent. It was in their interest to keep San Martín free to proceed on to Peru and to place a Chilean dedicated to the over-all plan in the new directorship. O'Higgins on all accounts was the likely choice. He was the ranking Chilean in the combined army, a close personal friend of San Martín, and a leading Chilean patriot. This is something that too many historians have seemed reluctant to acknowledge. O'Higgins represented the broad continental plan to the Argentines, and nationhood to the Chileans. He became Supreme Director because of a military feat, not because he had garnered the support of a reasonably large portion of the active citizenry, or of any part of it. Slightly over two hundred government officials and residents of Santiago elected him to the post as their second choice and in the early excitement of victory.

Once independence was declared officially and once the element of nationalism became a factor, especially after San Martín departed for Peru, O'Higgins became a less suitable national leader. By 1819 and 1820 O'Higgins began to remind Chileans more of their Argentine benefactor than their own national inviolability. This was the catalyst that activated the resentment of various segments of the population to his specific governmental actions. Alone, this animosity might or might not have caused his downfall, but in conjunction with his changed identity, at least as Chileans conceived it, it was too powerful a force to fail in achieving his overthrow.

CHAPTER V

The First Phase of Government

ON FEBRUARY 16, 1817, BERNARDO O'HIGGINS BECAME SUPREME DIrector of an administration that did not exist. Even before he could challenge the monumental problems facing him, he had to create administrative positions and locate competent people to fill them. All the royalists were turned out of office. Ministries had to be created and ministers found. Truly, a government had to be constructed in its entirety. Yet so pressing were the problems at hand that he proceeded to meet them even before his administration was intact. And there were indeed problems: The royalists still controlled a large portion of Chilean territory; the state was more or less without a treasury; and the Argentine troops were anxious to get on with their plan to invade Peru.

Three days after being appointed, O'Higgins decreed the confiscation of all royalist property. A central commission was established and then local commissions were added. An investigation of government financial resources was ordered. The results were desultory: Chile was poorer in 1817 than she had been in 1811. But money now began flowing in. Between the flight of Marcó and the end of April, the state's income was about 575,000 pesos. At the same time, expenses were only about 453,000 pesos. It was a favorable balance, but extremely misleading. The main bulk of the income did not come from ordinary sources; rather, it came from the seizure of royalist property. Nonetheless, the figures were inspiring. Even during the first days O'Higgins found enough money to institute reforms. On February 22 he ordered the establishment of a government newspaper and appointed Bernardo Vera its editor. He also took steps to establish a Chilean national army. Juan de Dios Vial was ordered to form "battalion number 1 of the army of Chile," the country's first infantry corps. Joaquín Prieto was given the task of forming the first artillery regiment. So great was the popular enthusiasm that both were filled in only a short while. A little later he decreed the establishment of a military school. Only graduates of the school could thereafter reach the rank of sergeant or higher. To head the school, O'Higgins selected Sergeant Major of Engineers Antonio Arcos. This is persuasive indication of the judicious calm with which the new Supreme Director was proceeding. Arcos was a Spaniard by birth, a factor obviously not held against him.

Further evidence of the imperturbable composure which characterized his early government is the tribunal he established to record the patriotic or unpatriotic activity of all Chileans during the reconquest years. Every Chilean was required to justify the label patriot. Yet those who did not qualify were not subject to exile or imprisonment. They might not be called upon to serve the government, but at least their person and property were inviolable. However, the property of non-patriots who refused to reside in Chile was subject to confiscation. One of his more controversial decrees had to do with the Church. He ordered the imprisonment of several friars who were especially determined in their opposition to the patriot cause. This was a direct infringement on ecclesiastical law. To make matters worse, O'Higgins even exiled the Bishop of Santiago to Mendoza and appointed his replacement.

But this is not to say that O'Higgins was omnipotent. He was a dictator in that he governed ostensibly without a legislature and could decree and enforce legislation. Yet the active citizenry expected the Director to act in accordance with the law. An illustrative example of the type of limitation placed on the Director's actions is the reaction of the *cabildo* of Santiago to O'Higgins' order that all Chileans vindicate themselves as patriots. The *cabildo* asserted that it did not care whether or not its members had received tribunal blessing for their previous activities. Several *vocales* did not even bother to appear before the tribunal, and the government ordered them to do so. The *cabildo* insisted that the *vocales* had been elected by the people, in whom resided the sovereignty of the State, before the law establishing the tribunal had been decreed. Thus, the *cabildo* reasoned, the public itself had qualified the *vocales* as patriots.[1] The *cabildo* took the day.

Perhaps the most significant development during his early days in office was the establishment of the *Logia lautarina* in Santiago. The impetus for its founding was furnished by San Martín, who determined to create a branch of the Buenos Aires lodge. It was a secret organization dedicated to the liberation of America. According to its statutes, any brother who revealed its existence would be punished by death. Should a brother become a government official he could not make any important decision without first consulting the lodge. In an emergency a brother could act as he saw fit, but under the condition that he would report his actions to the lodge. No brother in government could make any major appointment without lodge approval. That meant diplomats, governors of provinces, generals, justices, the high ecclesiastical officials, regimental chiefs of the army or militia, and others of this class.[2] Since no official lodge records exist, we cannot say precisely who actually belonged. Nor can we say what it actually accomplished. Certain it is that San Martín and O'Higgins belonged and that between February 1817 and the sailing of the expedition to Peru in August 1820 it was the power which governed Chile. Once the *Expedición Libertadora* and San Martín finally left Chile for Peru, the lodge no longer could justify its existence. And in fact, in terms of influence, it ceased to exist just at that moment. It was then that O'Higgins began to remind Chileans of the foreign origins of their independence and government more intensely than previously, something they preferred to forget.

While he was in the midst of organizing his government and preparing for the final thrust against the royalists in the south, O'Higgins received endless advice from friends and well-wishers. Two letters are particularly instructive for an appreciation of the complexity of his situation. In February 1817 the *mayorazgo* and recently Interim Governor, Francisco Ruiz Tagle, admonished him against believing that the triumph of arms would decide the luck of the American countries. "The Church and God will be the only ones that can make it triumph, because without the Church there is no government and without God, there are no good governors." [3] It is clear that not all patriots harbored anti-Church sentiments. During the same year the Bishop of Santiago, José Ignacio Cienfuegos, would say that the reason the American states had liberated themselves from the yoke of oppression was to re-establish the sacred rights the Almighty had conceded to man.[4] And he was appointed by O'Higgins. The Supreme Director had it early and on good authority that independence and the rights of man did not mean that the unique position of the Church should be altered. Yet in March he was urged by his long-time friend, the patriot-priest Juan Pablo Fretes, that he should "suffocate that aristocracy that already begins to raise its head. . . ." [5] Thus, an aristocrat told O'Higgins that the Church should be patronized, and a churchman told him that the aristocracy should be restricted. It is not surprising that before 1823 O'Higgins would offend each group.

Both O'Higgins and San Martín were convinced that the expulsion of the royalists from the south could be accomplished with little effort and in a short time. They conceived of the expedition to Peru as their main military task and agreed that the Argentine should travel to Buenos Aires to further consolidate the alliance between the two states and make final military arrangements. San Martín left Santiago on March 11, and before he returned in May, O'Higgins already had found it necessary to lead the southern forces personally. Early in April he wrote San Martín that things were not going well in the south. The troops were commanded by Argentine Colonel Las Heras, who, according to O'Higgins, was procrastinating and thus giving the advantage to the enemy. If the enemy held Talcahuano another twenty to thirty days, he noted, the winter would begin and the rains would favor a defensive action. He and the brothers of the *Logia* decided that he would go south to lead the troops. He expected to leave within a few days.

But it took him more time than he expected to arrange things in Santiago. He quite logically thought of Luis de la Cruz as his interim replacement. It seems that the *Logia* rejected this and proposed Argentine Colonel Hilarión de Quintana in his place. To carry out the liberation of Peru, to which he was dedicated, O'Higgins needed the support of Buenos Aires, and in a very real sense the *Logia* was that government's representative in Santiago. He was not in a position to hazard a break with either the lodge or Argentine government. But he did propose a compromise, one that reflected his experience in Mendoza. He suggested to the lodge that Quintana be given military command and that the Intendant of Santiago, Manuel Antonio Recabarren, be given political authority. This must have been rejected, since Quintana received both powers. That this occurred is both the measure of the *Logia*'s enormous powers and the degree to which the substance of the early O'Higgins government was not Chilean.

The public announcement of the temporary shift in government was made on April 15. O'Higgins must have suspected that it would cause considerable unrest, since he pointed out that he would be gone only a few days and that Quintana would govern with the aid of Chilean Minister of State Miguel Zañartu. On the following day O'Higgins departed for the south. He left a note for Quintana outlining sixteen things that the Interim Director should accomplish in the near future. Through subsequent messages to Quintana, O'Higgins made it certain that he was still Supreme Director. All along the route he occupied himself with the reorganization of the provincial regions he visited. To San

Martín he soon observed that all the towns of the two great provinces had been reorganized, that new governors had been appointed, commissions to supervise the sequestration of royalist property had been established, and that he had enforced "taxes—I mean loans—on the European Spaniards." [6]

He arrived in Chillán on the first of May. At once he found that members of the clergy were preaching against the government. He ordered Quintana to send patriotic clergymen.[7] In a few days he was in Concepción. He informed San Martín that the enemy in Talcahuano had recently received reinforcements of between five and six hundred men. But, he added with typical optimism, "Talcahuano ought to be ours shortly." Indeed, he was in good form. He was going to attack the towns of San Pedro and Arauco because they had been supplying the enemy. In closing he sent regards to the :::, as one brother of the *Logia* had to refer epigrammatically to the others. This was more than just wise diplomatic procedure; the brothers were his friends and compatriots-at-arms.

Now the patriot forces were having their first successes. On May 5 Las Heras defeated a superior enemy force. Two days later O'Higgins commended the Argentine's valor and military talents. He even praised his distinguished merit. This was kind of him, since his earlier remarks caused the Supreme Director of the United Provinces, Puerreydón, to order a military investigation of Las Heras' actions. On the eighth O'Higgins ordered part of his army to take the small strategic frontier town of Nacimiento. After that the troops had orders to proceed to their primary objective, the port of Arauco. The instructions he wrote indicated that the people of Nacimiento, just to the south La Laja, were to be treated with the greatest respect and consideration. But to enthuse the soldiers, the property of enemies in Arauco should be sacked. In a few days the troops, under the command of Lieutenant Colonel Ramón Freire and Captain José Cienfuegos, captured Nacimiento and gave the patriots control of both shores of the strategic Bío-Bío River. Now O'Higgins could limit the flow of food to Talcahuano from the south. At the same time he could supply himself from this new source. Almost immediately upon hearing of Freire's success O'Higgins asked him to send livestock to Concepción.

From the middle of May, O'Higgins' main concern was the capture of Arauco. He addressed a circular to its inhabitants which informed them that all of Chile from Copiapó in the north, to the Bío-Bío in the south was peaceful save for Talcahuano. And that port had no reason for hope.[8] Arauco could not have been convinced, since the town chose to fight. On the last day of the month O'Higgins told San Martín that Freire had taken Arauco, and that now Talcahuano's main point of supply from within Chile was closed. The rains were already slowing down all operations, and he hoped to commence the siege of Talcahuano as quickly as possible. Since the Chileans did not have a navy to blockade the port, all likely success rested with the army. O'Higgins often asked advice of San Martín, and he did again now. Early in June San Martín wrote O'Higgins that it would not be possible for Argentine naval forces to arrive in the Pacific in less than eight months. He told O'Higgins that since he knew the terrain and military circumstances he was fully authorized to do what he considered necessary.[9] This is a significant revelation. Apart from the fact that San Martín did not take the responsibility of ordering an attack on Talcahuano, he plainly authorized the Supreme Director of Chile to do what he thought best. This is another indication of the foreign character of the Chilean government. O'Higgins elected to attack the port.

While he was preparing to enter battle, O'Higgins had to devote considerable time to matters of government. Many reforms were decreed in May and June. He himself abolished coats-of-arms and other insignias of nobility. After the Battle of Chacabuco the engraver of the royal mint fled to Peru, and only an assistant with limited experience remained. Yet O'Higgins ordered that coins be minted. Thus it is that the first coins produced during O'Higgins' tenure carried the bust of Ferdinand VII. In June a more patriotic coin made its appearance. But the most interesting reforms were decreed without O'Higgins' approbation. Since many were limited to the capital itself, he may not even have been informed of them. A system of local mayors within Santiago was established to insure the central government direct control over every municipal quarter. This was designed both to inculcate patriotism and to provide order. The government decreed the hours that cafes, taverns, and billiard parlors could stay open, and in so doing shortened those hours. This is one of the puritanical measures for which O'Higgins was later criticized. A June decree made all crimes of robbery and assault subject to military justice. Special emphasis was placed on insuring public order. The death penalty was decreed for all robberies involving a value of four pesos or more. In cases involving less, the convicted would be sentenced to two hundred lashes and six years at hard labor. Though harsh, these were not unique measures for the era. Other reforms planned in the field of public education were stillborn through a general lack of funds.

So heavy were the rains during June that O'Higgins was confined to Concepción. Without supplies and activity troop morale was breaking. His Surgeon-General, the Englishman James Paroissien, had told him late in May that if the infirm—rheumatism especially always took a great toll at this time of year—did not receive better care, did not get such ordinary things as proper sheets, "the Motherland will not have anyone to defend it, at least in the Army of the South." [10] But the worst part was the confinement. To San Martín O'Higgins wrote in mid-June: "Already we are almost swimming with so much water; we are cut off on all sides. . . ." Even in July he was restricted to Concepción. Now his responsibilities in both the north and south were mounting. He ordered various officers to visit the southern Indian tribes, to renew old pledges of support and elicit new ones. Early in July Arauco fell to the enemy and Captain Cienfuegos, taken alive, was treated to a most barbarous death. By the middle of the month O'Higgins could report that Freire had retaken the strategic port.

While O'Higgins remained in the south, his replacement attempted to do the best he could in an anomalous position. Quintana was honest, hard-working, and of moderate abilities, but he was being pressured constantly by O'Higgins, San Martín, his ministers, and even the *Logia*. More than once he attempted to resign. O'Higgins wanted San Martín to assume the post, but the Argentine always refused. San Martín suggested Minister of War Zenteno, but he declined the offer. In turn, Zenteno suggested that a junta be appointed to replace Quintana. O'Higgins agreed and accepted Quintana's resignation. The new Junta, made up of Luis de la Cruz, Francisco Antonio Pérez, and José Manuel Astorga, was sworn in on September 7.

No appreciable change in the military situation occurred during September and October. The troops in the south continued to exist without supplies. In mid-October O'Higgins complained to San Martín that the soldiers had so little clothing that they could not partake even of exercises, no less a campaign. Though the rains had not yet ceased completely and the nights remained cold, he considered it now time to activate the siege against Talcahuano. Ships had been getting in and out of the royalist port all through the winter. But the rains continued, and expected supplies did not arrive. Toward the end of the month O'Higgins again observed to San Martín that it was time to begin the siege, but he was awaiting the arrival of six hundred rifles and clothing in order to undertake it.

It was during this period of inaction that O'Higgins signed the decree which created the Legion of Merit. The purpose was to honor those individuals whose contribution to the liberation of Chile was exemplary. As it turned out, the establishment of the Legion proved to be one of O'Higgins' most controversial acts. There was much world precedent for such an organization. The recent revolutions in what became the United States and in France produced similar bodies. And there was considerable pressure for it. Once the aristocratic coats-of-arms had been abolished, several influential citizens desired a republican replacement. And many of the patriot officers were foreigners who had served in European armies and had come to expect such reward for their service. Since the lodge brothers were to be affected more than any other single group, it is no wonder that the plan was approved with little difficulty. Members could be elected from among the military, civilian bureaucracy, Church, and private citizenry. Members received pensions and a special *fuero*—a right which stated that they could be tried only by the order, and not by the ordinary judicial procedure, for crimes of which they might be accused. O'Higgins named the first members, but thereafter the order became self-perpetuating. Very popular at first, the Legion of Merit soon developed an ardent opposition. It is not unusual for a historian to cite this as an example of O'Higgins' non-republican sentiments. The Legion of Merit was not a matter of republicanism, was not unique to Chile, and not unfamiliar to the times. Its purpose was precisely what the charter said: to honor those individuals who made special contributions to the new nation. There is no indication of any subterranean motives. The order endured until 1825.

Three days after he signed the Legion of Merit into existence O'Higgins sent a decree to Santiago which abolished all titles of nobility. So emotionally charged was the initial reaction of the Junta and other government officials that the decree was not published in the official newspaper until the end of November. This was O'Higgins' first major political blunder, especially because the active citizenry largely was predisposed against discordant social legislation. As a revolutionary statement it neither created nor added anything of value to the new nation. Prior to 1817 there were only twelve titled families in Chile, and ten had been royalist. But between the patriotic aristocrats and the royalists who remained in Chile, and by so doing protecting their property from expropriation, and their enormous families and relations, the titled aristocracy formed one central core of O'Higgins' support. O'Higgins never fully understood the nature of his power base or his relationship to it. Once the excitement of independence—still undeclared—diminished, the enemy expelled and San Martín departed for Peru, O'Higgins' permanence in office would depend on how carefully he had constructed his supporting foundation. Strategically it was less than desirable to alienate the powerful aristocracy so soon.

In early November the supplies O'Higgins so dearly needed began to arrive. On the eighth he informed San Martín that in a few days the army would march to Talcahuano. "The weather has calmed down and invites us to conclude the war." As usual his estimation of time was alarmingly imprecise. Eleven days later he remarked to San Martín that he had reviewed the troops in Concepción. Clothed in recently arrived unifoms, the army had taken on a remarkably promising appearance. In two days he intended to march to Talcahuano. He took the opportunity to note that the fighting along the frontier was bitter but that the patriots were winning. He thanked San Martín for the six hundred rifles he had just received and made it clear that he could use another three hundred. Finally on November 25 the army moved out of Concepción and headed toward Talcahuano.

It was not only war that occupied O'Higgins' attention during the fall and early summer of 1817. For some time now he had been concerned with diplomatic relations with European and other American nations. Early in April he had directed notes to various governments. To the United States he observed the similarity between the principles upon which both countries had been founded. He allowed that he was disposed to strengthen relations between the two countries and improve friendship and trade. To England he wrote that the new nation desired friendly relations most of all with this world power. After all, Chile had adopted a policy of freedom of trade, and England controlled the seas. There was no lack of diplomatic professionalism here. To the leaders of other governments, he pointed out that the ports of Chile were open to all friendly nations. The notes did not solicit recognition of independence since this still had not been declared.[11]

While planning the final assault on Talcahuano O'Higgins appointed José de Irisarri his Minister-Deputy to England and other European powers. He drew the instructions and signed them on November 24. Irisarri, in London at the time, was ordered to promote Chile in Europe and attempt to increase trade. It was his job to inform the European nations of the positive nature of the Chilean revolution for independence. Interestingly, he was instructed to encourage European immigration, assuring the Europeans that religious opinion would not be an obstacle. This was an attitude that O'Higgins would cultivate in later years, one that would cause him considerable trouble. By the time the instructions arrived in London, Irisarri was on his way back to Chile. Though he was not sent back to Europe immediately, some powers, most notably the United States, began to collect information about the little-known southern country and prepare their own future diplomatic policies.

The siege of Talcahuano commenced in earnest in December 1817. On the third O'Higgins reported to San Martín that he was firing one hundred and fifty rounds of cannon fire into the port each day. One could only imagine the miserable condition of that garrison in the last days. He expected to attack soon by sea with his launches and "by land, by different points." A few days later he noted that although the first assault was not fully successful it served to limit the enemy's freedom within the port. Every night the royalists treated the attackers to an incessant barrage of cannon fire. O'Higgins considered this a scared act, in fact, the act of a coward. "If they continue thusly, all the munitions of the fleet will not be sufficient." At the end of December he told San Martín that he expected an invasion of the province of Concepción. Yet the coast and most of the province were desolate of potential mounts and food supplies to support an invading army. He could not understand how the royalists might contemplate such an illogical move. "It is true that the Spaniards are very reckless in their military projects and perhaps ignorance blinds them." Nevertheless, the Spaniards did invade the province of Concepción, and under the leadership once again of General Osorio forced O'Higgins all the way back to Talca. At the end of January O'Higgins ordered the retreat of his army from the province under the protection of a rhetorical flourish aimed at the Chilean public. "The day of universal restoration is not far from us: this campaign is going to fix the destinies of Chile, and perhaps will fix also those of America."

In November Luis de la Cruz had written to O'Higgins indicating his belief that the Junta was not as effective in prosecuting the war as one individual might be. This is surprising since the

Junta had been most energetic in its support of O'Higgins and in assisting the country's economic development. Its attempts to stimulate the economy were intelligent and even daring. Export duties were lowered on selected items. In the hope that other nations would reciprocate, import duties were lowered also. A one per cent direct annual income tax was levied on all property owners. Liquid wealth was taxed likewise. To complicate matters for the Junta, the Chilean government had the responsibility of paying the salaries of the Army of the Andes ever since the Chacabuco success. At any rate, on December 10 O'Higgins ordered the Junta dissolved and invested its powers in Luis de la Cruz. Perhaps what prompted O'Higgins to disband the Junta was the rumor that Peru was mounting another invasion force to be sent to Chile.

Upon arriving in Talca O'Higgins received a draft of a declaration of independence sent by Luis de la Cruz. Late in 1817 a vote on the matter of independence had been taken throughout patriot Chile, and of the thousands who voted not one recorded a negative. O'Higgins refused the draft, and a new one was quickly drawn. This one he signed at Talca in February, but it was dated January 1, 1818 and read Concepción. It was a lengthy document that might well have arrived at the essence of its argument with these three lines:

> We want . . .
> We can . . .
> Then, we should be free.

At long last Chile was officially independent.

The patriots had just a month in which to prepare their defenses against the approaching enemy. They made their stand just to the north of Talca, at Cancha Rayada. It is interesting that San Martín now led the troops and that the Supreme Director merely served as an officer. In a surprising night attack on March 19, the royalists completely routed the patriots. O'Higgins was wounded in the right shoulder, but made his way back to Santiago. News of the disaster reached the capital on the twentieth. San Martín arrived on the twenty-second and attempted to lessen the disorder with promises that all was not lost and that the troops were gathering for a final defense. Captain Hill of the North American ship "Packet" described the day in his log: "On this day the confusion and despair in the city was extreme, many of the most influential men sent off their wives and families, and were preparing to follow themselves across the Andes toward Buenos Ayres, all the shops and stores were shut, and several officers of the government set out on their journey to abandon Chile." Hill, for one, did not lose his composure. To him it was incredible "that the finest army which Chile ever saw . . . had been thus entirely destroyed, and rendered incapable of making any further resistance against the advancing enemy. . . ." [12]

Obviously, not everyone remained as calm as Hill. Several influential leaders called for the establishment of a new junta with powers broad enough to meet the alarming situation. One of the more vocal advocates of this scheme was Manuel Rodríguez, perhaps the most romantic of all the independence leaders. Rodríguez had led the guerrilla forces in Chile during the reconquest, while other patriots like O'Higgins lived in safety across the border. His deeds certainly were already legendary. Cruz now granted him special powers to bring order to the capital. An assembly convened at eleven in the morning of the twenty-third, and by the afternoon had invested Rodríguez with even greater power. For nearly a day Rodríguez actually controlled the government of the capital. Charging about throughout the city, personally handing out sabers, he did stimulate morale. But O'Higgins arrived early in the morning of the twenty-fourth, and by his own decree reassumed his directorship. He had not planned to travel from the south to Santiago so soon. Loss of blood from his wound had weakened him considerably, but Minister Zañartu urged him to ride to Santiago to establish order regardless of his health. Against medical advice, O'Higgins rode in a forced march and arrived in Santiago in time to restore confidence.

While O'Higgins remained in the capital San Martín formed his forces on the plains of Maipo, just a few miles from the city. It took several days for the royalists to march as far as the Maipo. On the evening of April 2 San Martín began a moderate offensive movement which surprised the enemy, who expected that the patriot army, so recently defeated and so close to the capital, would be limited strictly to defensive actions. On the eve of the main battle, which occurred on the fifth, Santiago had all it could do to preserve sobriety. O'Higgins converted the capital into an armed camp, but residents rightly believed that the enemy could easily outflank the defenders and make their way to the capital. At nine in the evening of the fourth O'Higgins did receive a report that an enemy division had set out for Santiago. It appears that a suggestion was made that for his own safety he should join the main army, but O'Higgins chose to remain in Santiago. A royalist division did in fact start out for the capital, but could not find its way in the darkness, and returned to camp.

Sunday, the fifth of April, 1818, was one of those clear, cloudless days that seduces one into thinking the rains might come late this year. Each side had about forty-five hundred men, though the patriots possessed a larger cavalry and more artillery. Samuel Haigh, an Englishman, rode from the capital to the scene of the battle and recorded his observations.[13] At dawn Osorio mobilized his army and attempted to outflank San Martín and gain the road to Santiago. "San Martín immediately put his army into motion, and advanced toward the enemy, in close columns, and, by a rapid march, came upon them in time to frustrate this manoeuvre of occupying the main road." Osorio then took a position in front of a farm called Espejo. He deployed his two crack Spanish regiments on the right and left, leaving the center for the troops conscripted in Peru and Concepción. The center was flanked by divisions of dragoons and lancers. The patriots lined up in a similar fashion. The left was commanded by General Alvarado, the center by General Balcarce, and the right by Colonel Las Heras. The reserve was left to General Quintana. The fighting commenced about eleven o'clock, and by twelve the action was general.

At about this time the royalist left, the regiment of the Infantes of Don Carlos, descended its high vantage point and was riddled by patriot artillery. "The battle here was well contested, and remained a long time doubtful." The patriot cavalry then captured four pieces of royalist artillery, and "the guns were afterward turned against their former masters." Now commenced what was to be one of the bloodiest battles of the entire South American independence movement. The royalist right, the Burgos regiment, fired so effectively into the patriot left that it caused great confusion. Seizing their main chance the Burgos charged, but to their surprise the patriot reserves were at that moment brought up. The patriots won this encounter, and the Spaniards fled back to the hacienda Espejo. "They were pursued by the cavalry, and cut to pieces without mercy. Indeed, this virtue had been banished from the breasts of both parties. The carnage, was very great, and I was told by some officers who had served in Europe that they never witnessed any thing more bloody than occurred in this part of the field." In a short while both the royalist left and the center fell back to Espejo. "This farm has three court yards, and is surrounded by thick mud walls, capable of affording protection to two thousand men. . . ."

When the patriot army drew up before the hacienda it was greeted by a white peace flag. The royalists sued for a capitulation, and the patriots agreed. The gates were then blown open by cannon fire from within the courtyard, and the patriots charged in and killed without quarter. The royalists probably used a cannon as the simplest way of breaking down the barricade. There is no telling what the patriots just outside the walls thought. Hundreds of the defenders were killed in a few minutes. "The beautiful farm of the Espejo presented a dreadful picture after the action, its doors and windows perforated with musket balls; its corridors, walls, and floors, clotted and sprinkled with brains and blood; and the whole place, within and without, covered with dead bodies." It was a total victory. Shockingly few royalists ever made their way back to Talcahuano and then on to Peru.

That O'Higgins would remain in Santiago as the din of artillery fire resounded through the pulsating air was more than his physicians should have expected. He arrived in time to witness part of the battle. San Martín and O'Higgins "embraced, on horseback, and congratulated each other upon the fortune of the day." Haigh was in San Martín's company during most of the battle. It was he who carried word of the victory to Surgeon-General Paroissien. The chief medical officer sent Haigh to Santiago with a message requesting that wagons be sent at once to evacuate the wounded. The independence of Chile was now secure. At last the country was in a position to fulfill Simón Bolívar's 1815 prophecy:

> The Kingdom of Chile is destined, by the nature of its location, by the simple and virtuous character of its people, and by the example of its neighbors, the proud republicans of Arauco, to enjoy the blessings that flow from the just and gentle laws of a republic. If any American republic is to have a long life, I am inclined to believe it will be Chile. There the spirit of liberty has never been extinguished; the vices of Europe and Asia arrived too late or not at all to corrupt the customs of that corner of the world. Its area is limited; and, as it is remote from other peoples, it will always remain free from contamination. Chile will not alter her laws, ways, and practices. She will preserve her uniform political and religious views. In a word, it is possible for Chile to be free.[14]

Unfortunately, the Chile about which Bolívar was writing in 1815 had lost its freedom temporarily. Nevertheless, though their performance was exasperatingly uneven at times, Chileans, after Maipo in 1818, now began to justify the prediction.

With the royalist threat no longer a paramount question O'Higgins could stabilize his government, make the final effort to send San Martín and an invasion force to Peru, and inadvertently contribute to his own political end. Whereas O'Higgins represented the continental liberation movement as a whole, two Chileans personified primarily the Chilean national movement and managed to inspire patriotism and a national spirit as O'Higgins never could and never did. They were José Miguel Carrera and Manuel Rodríguez. Since the Argentine government supported O'Higgins, it was disposed against Carrera and his two brothers. Early in 1817 José Miguel arrived in Buenos Aires from the United States, and he was refused permission to proceed to Chile. Before the Battle of Maipo, Juan José and Luis Carrera attempted to make their way to Chile on the road through Mendoza. They were taken prisoner, and three days after the Chilean victory they were executed in Mendoza. The news was not well received in all Chilean circles, but certainly San Martín and O'Higgins appreciated that it was a fortuitous event. José Miguel was not executed in Argentina until 1821, but without his brothers his threat to the Chilean government diminished somewhat.

After the victory at Maipo, Rodríguez led his Hussars of Death in a hunt of fleeing royalists. In a matter of days O'Higgins ordered his detention. Rodríguez was taken under escort toward the town of Quillota, to the northwest of the capital. On the way he was killed by his guard. No event of O'Higgins' entire administration was less popular, and none has elicited more criticism by historians in later years. It is not perfectly clear whether he or the *Logia lautarina* ordered the murder. In either case there was collusion between the two; both feared the potential influence Rodríguez would have with the general population; both stood to gain; and neither was above such tactics. Rodríguez was thirty years old when he died. Samuel Haigh knew him "well, his sentiments were those of an ardent and virtuous free man." And indeed that was true. "He was, perhaps, the most popular man in Chile, but he differed on some points with the leaders of the government, which led to his melancholy end." [15] Of the Chilean heroes of the independence movement O'Higgins was now virtually alone. Those who had as much popular appeal—or even more—were either dead or moribund. But this was a spurious victory for O'Higgins, with somnolent overtones that induced him into thinking he had achieved a broad basis of support. The proclivity of most Chileans to support him while the country was underwriting an invasion of Peru further confirmed him in his opinion.

With the independence of Chile now firmly established, O'Higgins proceeded to give substance to the country's new status. Now the government sought recognition of independence from the United States and the European powers. The United States already had several agents in southern South America. Just four days after Maipo Special Agent John B. Prevost wrote to Secretary of State John Quincy Adams: "I now think the moment is fast approaching when it will become the policy of our government to recognize the independence of a great portion of South America and I again ask your attention to the incalculable sources of wealth which an ascendancy in the commerce of this Country offers to the U States." For its part, the Chilean government attempted to further this belief. A short while later Minister of Government Miguel Zañartu informed Special Agent W. G. D. Worthington, also of the United States, of Chile's enviable state of affairs: "We have no National Debt, and we already calculate on a Marine sufficient to govern the Pacific—free our Ports & ensure our enterprise against Lima. . . ." [16] But the bookkeeping continued to be fallacious: The books balanced because of property expropriations, not because the economy was flourishing.

But O'Higgins did not allow diplomatic rhetoric to lull him into the belief that the economy was doing well. Late in April he created a special commission to investigate the whole system of public treasury. A special commission was also appointed to supervise the expropriation of royalist property and to guard against fraud. Government income for the months of March and April together amounted to about 369,000 pesos, but expenditures were about 381,000 pesos. By combining existing surplus and debt the Ministry managed to balance the books. Yet this was still a surprisingly favorable situation. Things changed markedly in May. Income was now about 86,000 pesos. The drop was due largely to the short supply of property for expropriation. However, with the war effort ended, expenses were also down, to about 86,000 pesos. The main effort to outfit the *Expedición Libertadora* to Peru had not yet begun.

But by now Chile had already launched a naval war and engaged the enemy in what nearly proved a disastrous initiation. In early March the British frigate "Windham," owned by the East

India Company, anchored in Valparaíso. It had served its owners well, and now they would reap an extra profit by selling it as a potential warship. And indeed it had places for fifty cannons. A sale was arranged for 180,000 pesos. The government paid 105,000 pesos in cash, some of which seems to have come from a now ordinary source: patriotic contributions of household silverware and other items of value. Several foreign merchants in Valparaíso contributed another 25,000 pesos in return for participation in prize money brought in by the ship, and the government issued paper for another 50,000 pesos. In June the merchants were paid off in full by the government, which then owned the ship outright.

On April 26 the newly named "Lautaro" sailed from Valparaíso to capture the Spanish frigate "Esmeralda" and the brigantine "Pezuela," stationed to the south. Staffed by many of the sailors and officers who had brought it to Chile, the "Lautaro" engaged the two Spanish warships the following day. A timorous "Pezuela" sailed away from the battle. Thus, Captain George O'Brien could concentrate on the main target. He edged the "Lautaro" alongside the "Esmeralda," and with a handful of eager followers boarded her. O'Brien was killed along with several of his men, while others had to jump overboard to save their lives. While O'Brien was on the "Esmeralda" his own ship chased after the "Pezuela." It soon realized its mistake, but returned too late to save the day and the lives of those brave men. The "Lautaro" returned to Valparaíso safely, but it was not an auspicious beginning for the Chilean navy. However, there was some rejoicing in the fact that one Chilean ship had been bold enough to attack two Spanish ships and did in fact cause the questionable blockade of Valparaíso to be lifted. Even more, during this first voyage the "Lautaro" captured a small merchant vessel, the "San Miguel," which carried several royalist officers and private citizens. Two of the civilians ransomed their own freedom, and the government had enough money to pay for the outfitting of the "Lautaro," with enough left over to buy out its foreign partners in the ship.

O'Higgins and his advisers well appreciated the popular desire for a constitution. In early May, Special Agent Worthington presented the Supreme Director with his personal draft for a constitution for the new nation. But O'Higgins did not consider the moment propitious. First a census would have to be taken. In the meantime, he appointed a commission to draft a constitution that he intended to present to the constitutional convention that would convene in the future. Without an organic law to guide the nation O'Higgins found it necessary to clarify certain points that would have been covered by the constitution. Early in June he decreed that the term *chileno* would apply to all nationals of the country. Instead of the clause *Español natural de tal parte,* all official documents would use the term *Chileno natural de tal parte.* This applied to Indians also. As the decree stated, "it would be disgraceful to permit the use of formulas invented by the colonial system." But this was less altruistic than it appears. The internal class system was not modified. Hereafter the word *chileno* would refer to all nationals, including Indians, but "the formula that distinguishes the classes" was conserved. Excoriation of the term Spaniard was simply a matter of good patriotic sense. These were not democrats; it was not to be "Mr. Citizen" for everyone. Yet there were no inconsistencies between what the active citizenry thought and what it did. Problems of interpretation arise only when citizens of the twentieth century—some of whom delude themselves into thinking they are democrats—apply the democratic principles of Rousseau to citizens of the nineteenth century who were liberals and not democrats, and who found their ideological heritage in Locke and Montesquieu and perhaps Burke.

With the onset of winter O'Higgins' primary concern continued to be financial, but the country was stable enough for him to devote considerable attention to matters of public morality. In June he forbade card playing in public places. Less puritanical and more indicative of his liberal nature was a decree which abolished all fiscal duties on printed matter published in or out of the country. Yet the martial atmosphere cultivated by years of warfare persevered. On July 4 Worthington, one of Chile's most enthusiastic admirers, described this to Secretary Adams: "The Government itself is a complete military one—Everything is done by Soldiers—Even for the execution of a thief or a robber the soldiers are drawn out, formed around the place of execution, a sufficient section or Platoon, is drawn out and they fire upon the criminals. The Directoral Palace, as it is called, is guarded and thronged with soldiers—Instead of ordinary porters at the doors, soldiers with Bayonets receive you—The Director when he rides or walks out, has always on guard an escort of soldiers—In fine all the cities resemble military barracks and the country more or less is covered with soldiery."

In his letters to San Martín, now in Argentina, O'Higgins often noted the poor state of the public treasury. "Here we continue always harried by the lack of money; notwithstanding the army and the navy grow." Yet he considered the construction of public works important enough to undertake even though the treasury could ill afford them. No doubt he was inspired to such a position by the splendid example set by his father, but it was also a matter of national pride. He believed that public works gave a reliable indication of a country's level of civilization. In a July decree he accused Spain of neglecting Chile's public improvements to support its own court. But he was not thinking of improvements that would facilitate the traffic of goods or nourish the soil and crops, as did his father; rather, he was speaking about the construction of a public *paseo,* an avenue "where gentlemen can congregate for honest leisure and recreation in the hours of rest. . . ." This was not a question of the travails of establishing a government founded on a base of still inchoate political and economic rationales; it was a matter of good administrative judgment. O'Higgins thought this was a way of winning the support of Chilean gentlemen. And of itself it was, but conjoined with his anti-aristocracy and anti-Church decrees it served merely to divert precious funds from more beneficial improvements.

Yet one can understand that a novice political leader might be lavish in such things of personal prestige at a time when he might better have enhanced his public image through the construction of roads and canals. It must be noted, however, that work was being done on the Maipo Canal. For some time he had been having troubles with the Argentine deputy to Chile, Tomás Guido. In mid-July O'Higgins pleaded with San Martín to return to Chile to intervene in the matter. He felt that Guido's attempt to appear influential was allowing the impression that the Supreme Director was not his own man. O'Higgins was afraid that Chileans were forming the conclusion that their country was under the tutelage of Buenos Aires. His caution in the matter no doubt was prompted by a desire to avoid an open break with the Argentine government. While Guido and O'Higgins reached an accord by the end of August, the invidious impression already had been created. It was under these circumstances that the Supreme Director thought of public improvements that would be seen and enjoyed by many people, that would suggest the stability of the government and the resourcefulness of the Supreme Director.

O'Higgins had a penchant for orderly bureaucratic activity. In June he decreed that all government offices would be open between nine in the morning and two in the afternoon. They would open again between seven and nine in the evening. The Supreme

Director would hold a public audience every day except holidays and Thursdays, between ten and eleven in the morning. "In this audience there will be no preference for anyone." He also stipulated the exact half hours when his ministers could visit him. So crowded had his own schedule become that such orderliness was also a matter of personal survival.

The month of August was typical of the multiple activities which now consumed the Supreme Director's time, requiring his presence both in the capital and in Valparaíso. Early in the month he created a naval academy in Valparaíso to complement the military academy in Santiago. Once this was decreed, O'Higgins made an open appeal for books and instruments relating to naval science and mathematics—so basic were the country's needs. Chile lacked such necessities due to the "absurd politics of the Spanish Government. . . ." Also established in August was the *Sociedad De Amigos De Chile—Society of Friends of Chile.* Modeled after similar societies that had existed in other parts of America and Spain before the independence movement commenced, the Society was composed of leading members of society dedicated to improving all branches of the economy and all aspects of learning. Yet the organization had no authority in such matters. The Supreme Director named the first members. In the desire of establishing a public library O'Higgins appointed the learned Manuel de Salas to the post of national librarian, charged first with cataloguing the books held by the consistory of San Carlos. On August 8 he made it perfectly clear that the Supreme Director inherited the Patronato Real, the royal patronage over the Church. He would nominate Church officials to be approved by the Papacy, and he would decide what Church documents could be made public, including papal bulls. On this date he removed from office a Church official who was obdurate in his opposition to the new government, and replaced him with someone more amenable.

As if he were not busy enough he found it necessary to travel to Valparaíso. On the twenty-seventh he informed San Martín that he would proceed to the port within three days "to agitate the equipping of the *Lautaro,* the ship *General San Martín* (alias the *Cumberland*), the sloop *Chacabuco,* and the brigantines *Pueyrredón* and *Arauco.*" It was a formidable little fleet, having been created so recently. O'Higgins wanted to get it out to sea in time to intercept an expedition that was rumored to be leaving Cádiz.

While O'Higgins was occupied in Valparaíso, he received San

Martín's resignation. The General's health was failing, but O'Higgins would not hear of resignation. "San Martín is the hero destined for the salvation of South America," he announced to San Martín on September 20, "and you cannot renounce the preference that eternal Providence has indicated." O'Higgins was rather pleased with the fleet, expecting the main part to put out to sea in four days. And it was the fleet that required the Minister of Treasury to demonstrate considerable skill and ingenuity in balancing his books. Though he managed to do so each month, expenditures were increasing with revenues not keeping pace. In July the government took in slightly over 159,263 pesos, but spent over 162,159 pesos. Military costs were going up, but the largest single rising category was naval expenses. For July they were about 42,512 pesos. In August naval expenses reached an alarming 112,101 pesos. It is not surprising, then, that in September the government stepped up its program of property expropriation and disposal.

Toward the end of September it looked as though the fleet would soon be able to sail. O'Higgins took the somewhat contemptuous step of closing for one month all Chilean ports to further traffic. This meant that ships presently at port could not leave and those at sea could not dock. This was done to facilitate the fleet's task of seeking out the enemy. But it did not endear the Supreme Director to foreign and domestic shippers and merchants. On October 6 O'Higgins informed San Martín that in two days the fleet would set sail. It was now well staffed and supplied with enough food for four months. The fleet could not depart earlier for lack of funds. It had even been necessary to obtain food by force, "but the entire body of officers (which is very good) goes paid." Though later than O'Higgins predicted, the fleet finally sailed. The exact date is not certain, but it was probably the ninth. O'Higgins returned to the capital in time to celebrate the adoption of the provisional constitution, the first one for the independent nation.

The special commission appointed by O'Higgins had drafted the document, which was then sent throughout the country for a vote. The vote was by municipality, and not a negative was cast. It was a provisional document promulgated by the Supreme Director, and it went into effect on October 23, 1818. Until a Congress be called, and as it turned out that was not for several years, the legislative branch would comprise only a Senate of five members, selected by the Supreme Director. They were to receive substantial annual stipends of two thousand pesos, but were forbidden to hold other public employment. Any citizen more than thirty years old, "of exalted patriotism, of integrity, prudence . . ." was eligible for membership. The only serious qualification was age. Since members of the active citizenry were going to elect government officials from among their own number, no more specific qualifications were necessary. Democracy was not an issue at the moment, and as a political ideology had few if any articulate supporters. The primary purpose of the Senate was to insure observance of the constitution. It was given the broad and effective powers that a legislature should possess in a republican form of government. Senate approval was required on all important matters, such as "imposing taxes, soliciting loans, declaring war, making peace, forming treaties of alliance, commerce, neutrality; sending ambassadors, consuls, deputies or envoys to foreign powers; raising new troops or sending them outside the State; undertaking public works and creating new authorities or employs." The Senate could pass a law over the Supreme Director's veto. Provision was made for amending the constitution.[17]

This is a much misinterpreted document. Historians have been all too eager to form their opinions about the constitution on the basis of one point. The Senators were not elected; they were appointed by the Supreme Director. As the serviceable syllogistic argument would have it, it follows therefore that the Supreme Director in reality created a specious legislature to lend respectability to his regime. It is often suggested that O'Higgins reserved unlimited powers for himself. At best this may have been his intent. There is little evidence to indict or absolve him on this point. However, as it turned out, the Senate proved to be a viable, energetic legislature.

The constitution provided that the present Supreme Director would continue his tenure, but in the future Directors would be elected by the provinces. Qualifications for the position were similar to those of the Senate. The Supreme Director's privileges were the standard and familiar ones. The constitution divided Chile into three provinces: Santiago, Concepción, and Coquimbo. An independent judiciary was established. The customary contemporary civil liberties were guaranteed. The congressional decree declaring children born to slaves to be free was repeated. But there was no special section on citizenship. Nothing was included to eliminate the Indian from citizenship. In a negative manner, the document thus granted that citizenship. Everyone was instructed to follow this moral principle: *No hagas a otro lo que no quieres hagan contigo.*

On this solid constitutional base both Supreme Director and Senate began to act. O'Higgins dispatched Irisarri to London, charging him to secure recognition of independence from Russia, Great Britain, the United States, or Holland. Recognition by any of these was considered decidedly advantageous. Irisarri's instructions have become a point of excessive controversy. One article instructed him to assure the European powers that in the near future Chile would adopt a moderate constitutional monarchy. They have become controversial not because it would appear that O'Higgins had a predilection for monarchy, but because they were never signed or confirmed.

Thus, one is able to speculate purely on the basis of circumstantial evidence whether or not O'Higgins was a monarchist at heart. It was hardly an oversight: The Supreme Director drafted the instructions in a way that they would better serve as an efficacious instrument of diplomacy. And he did so in a way that he could stand by them if pressure for a monarchy were to be applied from Europe. Yet there is the possibility that he left them unsigned so that he would not have to defend the monarchical plan to the United States. In fact, later O'Higgins did disclaim any interest in monarchy, asserting that he was a republican.[18] And this he was, but the idea of a monarchy was not insufferably abhorrent to him. It was, after all, a rather accepted and respectable institution in Europe and was not entirely incompatible with his own political concepts. Yet he claimed to be a republican, and when in a position to establish a monarchy he never did. And he declined to do this when the government of the United Provinces of Río de la Plata manifested a strong interest in monarchy, when many of his own supporters, especially San Martín and several other members of the *Logia lautarina,* desired a monarchy, and when he might well have become the monarch. When Irisarri arrived in San Luis early in 1819 after having crossed the Andes en route to Buenos Aires, he noticed that the instructions were unsigned, and he immediately requested that this be done. It never was done.[19]

In early November the Senate abolished the *consulado* and the *tribunal de minería,* the commercial and mining tribunals. For such an unprecedented and potentially disruptive act, it asked the Supreme Director's approbation. This was given in a short time. It also re-established the Instituto Nacional, under the same rules and conditions upon which it was founded in 1813. The nation's leading secondary school was thus reopened after having been closed by the royalists. While the Senate was deliberating over such matters, news of the greatest moment reached the capital.

On November 9 the *Gaceta Ministerial* announced that the "San Martín" and "Lautaro" had captured the Spanish frigate "Reina María Isabel." The fifty-cannon warship was taken near the port of Talcahuano. The news, as Agent Worthington related it to Washington, "has been received with great rejoicing here—On the night of the news the Supreme Director gave a Splendid Ball at which I took occasion to say to Genl. San Martín, that I supposed some of those *circumstances* had occurred which would enable him to say when they would go against Lima." It is a commentary on the nature of the new government's relationship with the Church that San Martín, recently returned to Santiago, was quartered in the Bishop's Palace. The exploits of the small fleet continued to excite patriotic imagination. At about eleven in the evening of November 17, word reached the capital that several Spanish transports, formally protected by the "María Isabel," had been taken. "The congratulations to the Supreme Director & the rejoicing on the occasion," Worthington reported the following day, "were of the most lively cast—Today the official report is that three large transports originally carrying 600 men are the Prizes." The patriots were sure now that the few remaining royalist troops would be forced to leave the country momentarily.

It was just in the wake of these early naval successes that Lord Cochrane, the most famous European in the Latin American independence movement, arrived in Valparaíso. The Chilean agent in England, Alvarez Condarco, had made arrangements for Cochrane to join the Chilean navy the year before. Thomas Cochrane, tenth Count of Dundonald, was born in Scotland in 1775. At seventeen he began his naval career, and before twenty-five he was captain of the brigantine "Speedy," a small ship with under a hundred men and officers. His assignment was to attack enemy ships independently of the fleet. Taking advantage of his speed and slight draft, Cochrane terrorized enemy shipping for three months. By the time he was captured by three French vessels, he had taken somewhere around fifty ships, over a hundred cannons and more than five hundred prisoners. Through a prisoner exchange he managed to return to Great Britain, where he soon entered Parliament. Too liberal for his party, arrangements were made to give him command of the frigate "Imperieuse." His daring exploits once again brought him success and fame. It seems that Napoleon remarked: "Cochrane would have been able to destroy or take all the French ships, if, as he should have done, the English admiral would have helped him." [20]

Soon he was back in Parliament. He was indeed a popular representative, but the Chilean purchasing agent made his contact just as Cochrane had suffered the humiliation of a national scandal. Once he agreed to fight for Chilean independence, he ordered the construction of a steam warship. It was completed in July 1818, but it could not make enough steam to travel. Rather than wait for adjustments to be made, Cochrane proceeded to Chile. He arrived in Valparaíso on November 28, 1818. Soon thereafter Worthington described him to Adams: "He is about 40 years old, very tall and not corpulent, rather of a Stripling appearance; not courtly in his address, but very plain and bold in his remarks and opinions; Yet not authoritative nor pompous. . . ."

O'Higgins greeted Lord Cochrane personally in Valparaíso. There followed at once a series of parties first at the port and then in Santiago. Cochrane later recorded his impression of the first days: "The same scenes were, however, re-enacted at the distant capital, whither the Supreme Director insisted on taking us, till I had to remind His Excellency that our purpose was rather fighting than feasting." He was very pleased with the Chilean squadron, which had just returned from the successful cruise during which the "María Isabel" had been captured: "The squadron consisted of the recently captured Spanish frigate, now named the *O'Higgins* . . . the San Martín, 56 guns, formerly the Cumberland Indiaman, which had been bought into the service; the Lautaro, 44 guns, also a purchased Indiaman; the Galvarino, 18 guns, recently the British sloop of war *Hecate;* the *Chacabuco,* 20 guns; and the *Arauco,* 16 guns; a force which, though deficient in organization and equipment, was very creditable in the energy of a newly emancipated people." [21] Cochrane was given the rank of vice-admiral with a salary of six thousand pesos and declared first in command of the Chilean navy. Manuel Blanco Encalada, fresh from his triumphs against the "María Isabel," and later President of Chile, was made rear admiral and second in command.

Still in November O'Higgins established with the approval of the Senate various new and higher taxes. With plans for the liberation of Peru going ahead so surprisingly well, with San Martín back in Santiago and Cochrane in Valparaíso, and the timely capture of part of the Spanish fleet, O'Higgins was in a position to raise taxes and yet count on popular support for his administration.

But this did not include influential elements within the Church. Special Commissioner of the United States to South America Theodorick Bland described the impecunious situation to Adams in November: "The present patriot authorities, owing to the nature of the revolution itself, to their prodigality, to their having too many hungry expectants about them, or to some other causes, are continually pressed for resources." Bland was particularly concerned about the government's attitude toward the Church: "They have repeatedly cast an eye upon the accommodations and the wealth of the church. They have solemnly asked the opinion of the holy fathers as to the propriety and policy of raising a considerable sum of money by the sale of bulls and indulgences; and were answered that neither right nor religion would forbid it." As Bland noted, the government had "seized upon two large monasteries, turned out the monks to seek accommodation elsewhere among their brethren, and made barracks of the holy lodgings." He seemed somewhat appalled by the treatment of the religious themselves. "They have tried and convicted monks and *nuns* of high treason, and sent them into banishment. . . ." He also reported, with equal accuracy, that the government had borrowed the ecclesiastical census in order to establish its own tax scale. And indeed it was an effective tool with regard to both the religious and lay communities.

Shortage of funds continued to undermine the government's efforts to mount an invasion of Peru during the new year. For O'Higgins this penury was taking on the character of a leitmotif. Early in January 1819 he determined to suspend temporarily the Military Academy as part of an austerity program. Approval by the Senate was forthcoming without delay. He also requested the Senate to approve the elimination of various high ranks from the military officialdom, arguing that the exhaustion of the public treasury, the nation's nascent state of development, and the size of the military establishment did not warrant too many high ranks and pompous titles. Therefore, he suggested that the classes of marshal be abolished. And this in light of the fact that recently he had been elevated to the rank of great marshal by the same Senate. The only rank of general that would be permitted was that of colonel-general, "but without more salary, rewards or treatment than the simple Colonel." Likewise, the rank of admiral was eliminated from the navy, leaving only rear admirals and vice-admirals at the highest level. And this the Senate approved. It was an audacious step for O'Higgins to take just at a time when Chile had not yet rid herself of all royalist opposition in the south, and when the war against Peru was still pending.

As Worthington prepared to return to the United States he arranged a final meeting with the Supreme Director that proved to be notably instructive to the Special Agent. He offered to convey any message to the President that O'Higgins thought better not to present in writing. The Supreme Director answered "that they should have been highly gratified if the United States had thought proper to have recognized their independence." Obviously, O'Higgins no longer was attempting to solicit recognition through some indirect diplomatic rhetoric. Worthington then asked O'Higgins what kind of government he intended to establish. "Do you intend to have any kind of Monarchy? He unhesitatingly replied—That they intended to have a confederated Republican form of Government." As Worthington reported it, O'Higgins stated that "as soon as Peru is emancipated we hope that Buenos Ayres and Chile and Peru will form one great confederation similar to that of the United States." Certainly, O'Higgins would not have advocated monarchy to the representative of the United States even if privately he entertained such an idea (which at any rate is not at all clear). It is more than likely that by 1819 O'Higgins had settled upon the republican form of government as offering Chile the greatest advantages. It would mollify any fears harbored by North Americans concerning the predilection of Chileans for a monarchy, and at the same time—because republicanism and democracy were not necessarily synonymous—a strong government could be established that would be appealing to the European powers.

As the summer came and went, the Chilean plans for the invasion of Peru were jeopardized by mordant instability in the United Provinces of Río de la Plata. Supreme Director Pueyrredón vigorously advocated a monarchy, but not all Argentines agreed with him. To make matters worse, José Artigas, on the eastern shore of the Plate River in what was soon to become Uruguay, was an ardent republican with an urge to revolutionize, one who represented to many an alluring alternative. Perhaps most unsettling of all was Pueyrredón's belief that the Spaniards were about to send another invasion force from Cádiz, this one to the Plate estuary. At the same time, San Martín was not pleased with the way in which things were working out in Santiago. In mid-December 1819 he had requested 280,000 pesos from the Chilean government to mobilize the *Expedición Libertadora* to Peru. The Senate refused to concede the sum, indicating that the treasury already had made sizable contributions to the venture and could not afford further financial burdens. The statement was not couched in diplomatic terms; no effort was made to suggest that the treasury would be able to afford such expenditures in the future. This unexpected action provoked San Martín into a pique that was not assuaged even when the Senate later approved a smaller sum. The General-in-Chief of the *Expedición Libertadora* did not suffer the Senate's spontaneous autonomy alone. In January 1820 the Supreme Director presented a routine budget for naval stores, and the Senate refused to accept it.

So disenchanted was San Martín by the Senate's intransigence that he proposed that Buenos Aires recall the Argentine troops stationed in Chile. This coincided precisely with Pueyrredón's own wishes. Early in March the order was given. Upon hearing of it the Argentine deputy in Chile, Guido, wrote to San Martín imploring him to keep the troops in Chile. He challenged Pueyrredón's argument point for point. The combined invasion force was not comprised of four thousand Argentines and one thousand Chileans as the Director stated. Rather, it was two-thirds Chilean; and even if most did not desert on the way home, their absence from Chile would open the country to attack. More, this would allow the Spaniards to attack the United Provinces from various points. That is, with a strong army in Chile, the Spaniards would have to defend the borders of Peru, and would be less likely to strike out on the offensive from Peru. Guido also discounted the ancillary argument that the suspected invasion from Spain was pertinent here. He suggested that it was at least six months off, and that its future actually depended on the strength of Peru. Pueyrredón had posited his argument on the assumption that the *Expedición Libertadora,* at any event, was not ready to leave for Peru. Guido answered that the expeditionary force in fact was prepared to leave momentarily.[22]

O'Higgins was not initially so sure as Guido. At first he wrote to San Martín that it would be a terrible thing to move the Army of the Andes across the cordillera and expose Chile to attack, but if Pueyrredón was sure of the invasion from Spain no other recourse remained but to send the troops back. But the *Logia* was inexorable in its opposition to the withdrawal. Two days before Guido wrote his letter to San Martín, O'Higgins sent one indicating that the O—O, as the brothers at times referred to the lodge epigrammatically, had resolved to send one of the brothers to deliver a verbal message to San Martín. It is evident from the letter that the O—O had decided to keep the Army of the Andes in Chile for a while longer, at least, that is, until news arrived concerning the fate of the fleet now patrolling the Pacific under the command of Cochrane. On March 18 the Senate ruled that the Army of the Andes must remain in Chile under the present circumstances. Thus on the following day O'Higgins wrote to San Martín informing him that a letter was about to leave for Buenos Aires telling Pueyrredón that the troops would remain in Chile. The Supreme Director was at his diplomatic best. He noted the grave danger that Buenos Aires faced if the Spanish invasion should materialize; but the Senate would have to approve the sending of troops out of the country, and this it failed to do. O'Higgins told the General-in-Chief that he was going to abide by the Senate's decision, and the decision taken also by the O—O. This was not merely a diplomatic ruse: O'Higgins had two powerful partners in the government of Chile. Neither the *Logia* nor the Senate was submissive to the wishes of the Supreme Director, and their patent independence further suggests the dualistic nature of the Chilean government.

The disinclination of the Senate to indulge the Supreme Director is illustrated by another of its actions precisely at the time it reached a decision concerning the removal of Argentine troops. Acting under advice from one of his commissions, O'Higgins sent a resolution to the Senate that proposed to establish an additional tax on real estate. The Senate refused to approve it. In a lucid note the Senate persuasively argued that Chile was an agricultural country, that those dedicated to agriculture already bore the central burden of taxation. And not only in the financial sense; they also supplied the food and animals required by the armed forces. Yet O'Higgins was not convinced; he insisted that the Senate approve the measure. For its part, the Senate stood fast and refused to be intimidated. Even under the contingencies of war and the divisive Argentine threat, the Senate proved more than the Supreme Director could manage.

This querulous independence on the part of the Senate should not conjure up an image of representatives of a landed aristocracy acting invidiously on its behalf. In this case, the interests of large and small landholders were similar. All suffered from the inequitable system of taxation. As the Senators noted, most of the commercial operations in the country were controlled by foreigners, who as yet were not required to contribute directly to the general welfare of the state. Perhaps the Senators were merely suggesting a shift in the burden of taxation. The British merchant community had established the precedent of taking up a subscription on behalf of the government. In mid-April the Senate ordered the Supreme Director to convoke separately the merchant communities of the United Provinces and North America for the purpose of informing them of the country's financial situation and the trade advantages that would accrue to them through the liberation of Lima. The Supreme Director was authorized to request of these alien communities a voluntary contribution. Thus ended the solitary financial burden so far withstood by the agricultural community.

So far, the Chilean government had done nothing physical to prevent the withdrawal of Argentine troops. Toward the end of March, O'Higgins reported to San Martín that still he had not heard from Cochrane. Early in April a messenger from San Martín told the *Logia* that San Martín had agreed to its resolution and would not send troops back across the cordillera. O'Higgins rejoiced in the decision. As well he might, since the alternative would have seriously undermined the alliance between Chile and the United Provinces, now on a formal basis, and also would have jeopardized the liberation of Peru. On the same day that O'Higgins informed San Martín of his delight over the latter's decision, he observed in a second letter that desertions in the Army of the Andes had been great. Major contingents of the Army had been idle too long, and word that the Argentines had been ordered home by Pueyrredón played havoc with order. Ten days later O'Higgins informed San Martín that segments of the Army of the Andes stationed in northern Chile had grouped for the trip across the cordillera. News of this had engendered further desertions.

Just as it appeared that the cherished continental dream was to perish from atrophy, word reached Santiago of the splendidly irreverent Lord Cochrane. Under the cover of fog he had sailed intrepidly directly into the port of Callao, within easy reach of shore batteries, and attacked the Peruvian fleet. As if to enhance his reputation as a daring admiral, he sailed, at least as it turned out, into the Viceroy's cannon fire with a single ship. Cochrane did little damage, and, it would seem, was lucky to rejoin his own fleet safely. The fact is he was not noticeably successful at all during this first voyage. For his efforts all he could show was the several merchant vessels he had captured. But his exploits charged the imagination of a receptive Chilean audience. Cochrane had even declared the port of Callao and the coast of Peru under blockade. This more than anything else stirred the Chileans to greater patriotism. However, news of the fictitious blockade was less ecstatically received in Europe. "I expect grand things of this man very shortly," O'Higgins exulted. Now it was O'Higgins' turn to sponsor the continental plan, to arouse his colleagues. To San Martín, still recovering from senatorial abuse, he wrote: "It is necessary not to forget that without the liberty of Perú there is no permanent independence." Yet it took nearly a year and a half for the *Expedición Libertadora* to depart for Peru.

Lord Cochrane had sailed with the Chilean fleet to Callao in the middle of January 1819, and a short while later the war against the remaining royalist troops in the south was brought to a temporary conclusion. However, in August there was a resurgence in southern royalist might, and the royalist leader, Benavides, called for the *total exterminación* of the patriots. Thus commenced the famous War to Death that did not end for several years. The *modus vivendi* of the O'Higgins government, that is, the informal accord reached by the government of the United Provinces with O'Higgins and the Chilean public concerning a government for Chile, already began to suffer from disaffection on the part of many Chileans. And this commenced quite a time before the invasion force actually sailed for Peru in August 1820. Late in January 1819 Worthington, who was distinctly fond of O'Higgins, recorded his incisive observations on the question of the Supreme Director's popularity: "I think he has lost the Love and Confidence of the Nation—they think him a political automaton, & that too, playing upon his own native country. . . . He may continue chief Magistrate of Chile for some years to come, but he must have an armed power to Support him & that not even a Chilean one." Worthington understood very well the nature of O'Higgins' rise to power: "For the great Paternal popularity, the splendid hereditary reputation, which enshrouded him, as he stepped forth, the champion of his country's rights have faded away and left only a tinsel, military pageantry in their stead." And then, as if to presage the line taken by later apologists, he added: "It may be possible, he thinks he is doing right all this time, and acts for the good of his country. I don't think so & I suspect Posterity will coincide with me."

During the spring of 1819, while popular attention focused on the fractious Army of the Andes and the inspiring Lord Cochrane, the government proceeded with the consolidation of its gains and the establishment of what it considered a liberal government. One of the more important pieces of legislation to be proposed by the executive branch and approved by the legislature during the year pertained to public education. A law was passed providing for the creation of public schools throughout the country. The schools were required to instruct Chilean youth in reading, writing, and counting, with special emphasis to be placed on the learning of Spanish grammar. In addition, the pupils were to be instructed in the "fundamentals of our sacred religion, and the christian Doctrine . . . ," which was rather more a measure of the inherent religiosity of the government leaders than their desire to propitiate the Church fathers for past impiety. Without mentioning the Indian by name, O'Higgins decreed in March that these members of society were citizens and were entitled to complete freedom and equality. Legally this was repetitious; it had been stated before. It was probably restated now due to an interesting consequence of citizenship. In late February the Senate ruled that since the constitution raised the indigenous population from the condition of slavery and converted it to citizenship, those included in this category would have to fulfill the ordinary responsibilities of citizenship. That is, they would have to serve in the armed forces. Under such circumstances it is not surprising that O'Higgins would find it advisable to reiterate the fact of citizenship, which was manifestly less tangible to the Indian than military service.

Other measures were more obviously liberal in motivation. The 1813 law which governed the press, and in fact all publications, was reinstated, and with it the ubiquitous Junta of Censure, whose members were appointed by the government. One might correctly argue that in this manner controls were placed on the publication of private opinion. However, as in 1813 the goal was to attain to a state of free press by applying controls that would eliminate reckless slander and bring not only freedom to the writer and publisher, but protection to the individual or organization at whom the statements were directed. The element of censure would have been repulsive to a democrat, were there one in Chile during the period. The government had approved a solicitation presented by a Swede, Johan Adam Graaner, which would allow him to send foreigners into Chile to enter the mining industry in all its varied aspects. In March O'Higgins decreed that residents of any nation and believers of any religion sent by Graaner would be welcome and would fall under the government's protection. However, the Swede soon died, and the franchise was not implemented.

This intent to attract competent foreigners regardless of their religious persuasion was one of O'Higgins' most progressive and laudable traits. But in his attempt to reform he never correctly gauged the desires and needs of a society just beginning to feel the security of a costly independence and still under the burden of its obligation to a continental plan of liberation not of its own making. O'Higgins was an incomparably dedicated man who enjoyed few luxuries and little leisure. He expected all Chileans to warrant a similar description. As a revolutionary leader who had been called upon by his fellows to lead them to freedom, which he was, this attitude was appropriate, but as a political leader who intended to remain in power longer than necessary to establish a stable government, which he did, it was tactically ill-advised and further weakened his support among various sectors of society. In May he decreed that all categories of card games were prohibited absolutely. This was unpopular enough, but to compound the error he added that this ruling pertained to games in private homes as well as public places.

In June there appeared an editorial in the *Gaceta Ministerial* which could serve as a political manifesto for the O'Higgins government. The *Gaceta*'s editor was Bernardo Vera, born in the Viceroyalty of Río de la Plata (some say that he was born in Mexico and raised in La Plata), but who emigrated to Chile when he was nineteen. It is very likely that he wrote this particular editorial. It commenced with a declaration of the four basic rights of man: "liberty, property, security and equality. . . ." Then followed a lengthy discussion of each right. So far as liberty is concerned, the writer observed that he was speaking about civil liberty, which must not be confused with natural liberty, because this last authorizes one to do good or bad, and "easily degenerates into license." As for equality, it "is the right to invoke the law in your favor, the same for the rich as the poor, the large and the small." But this is not to say that all have the same laws. There are and should be different laws regulating "the clergy, the military, the simple citizen, the wards of the state, the aged, etc., etc." By equality this writer meant civil not natural equality, that all men had the right to act as freely as they chose, just so they did not trespass on the freedom of their fellows; that every man could invoke the full protection of the law as it pertained to his class. And the various classes of society do not oppose this legal equality: Far from that, they conserve it because without the class structure there cannot be order, and without order there is no society. Emphasis was placed on not confusing natural rights with civil rights. Security was dealt with briefly, since it after all is merely the right of not being violated, and not being the victim of government caprice. Likewise property, which is man's prerogative to be the owner of his person, of his industry, of his talents, and of the fruits that accrue through his work.

While it is not possible to ascertain just how closely O'Higgins adhered to the concepts expressed in this editorial, one must consider the fact that it appeared in the government's official newspaper. Though O'Higgins does not seem to have been particularly concerned with the justification and preservation of a class structure, he held a similar view of liberty, equality, security, and property. He was, as much as the writer of the editorial, a classical liberal and a non-democrat. In light of this conception of rights, as Edmund Burke said, the real *rights,* the question of monarchy becomes almost meaningless. Monarchy was not at all alien to the society depicted by these nineteenth-century liberals. In fact, the two were entirely compatible. Yet it must be remembered that such liberals could still be republicans. That is, they could and generally did prefer a government composed of three branches and a system of effective checks and balances. That they chose to establish a republican form of government without a monarchy is not a measure of their dedication to republicanism, for monarchy and republicanism were not mutually exclusive terms, nor of their democratic principles, for they were not democrats. It is simply that they were impressed by the North American example and aware that a monarchy would lessen the chances of obtaining recognition from that republic, that they had just fought a war against a monarch and appreciated that monarchs were losing their vogue in Europe, and that they perceived no particular advantage of having a monarchy in their liberal republic. In later years when monarchs fell into a deeper and more permanent disrepute, the image of José Miguel Carrera, who indeed was less inclined toward monarchy, would grow at the expense of liberals like O'Higgins.

During the winter of 1819 the government proceeded along a course chartered now quite some time ago. When the Senate had abolished the merchant tribunal it gave as its excuse the critical shortage of funds. In its stead was created a *Juez de Comercio*—a commercial judge. This served to take control of commerce out of the hands of the merchants. At the behest of the merchant community the Senate re-established the tribunal, but under the condition that it be financed by the merchants themselves. Money was clearly the central issue so far as the government was concerned, but the Senators doubtless had taken into consideration the royalist implication of the tribunal when they first abolished it. Now that independence was secure, this probably was less an issue. Since 1810 government officials were actively considering methods of circumventing the traditional and unsanitary practice of burying the dead within the Church edifice itself. Now at last something was done about the matter. In August the Senate actually ordered the construction of new cemeteries. It was more than just a matter of public health: With open cemeteries away from the Church buildings and property, arrangements might be made to accommodate the needs of non-Catholics. Burial of non-Catholics heretofore, with restrictions on public practice of another religion, was considered somewhat of a disreputable affair. This was, therefore, an important step in preparing a harmonious environment for foreigners. It is interesting that the Senate invoked an 1804 royal decree ordering the construction of cemeteries for precedent, an indication of both security and maturity.

It was during this same winter that the government began to receive the first important notices from Irisarri, its representative in Great Britain. Irisarri had arrived in London displaying boundless optimism. Since his primary goal was to secure recognition, he set out to impress the London community. He quartered himself well, rode around town in a fine carriage replete with liveried coachmen, and proposed to invite influential people to his residence. All this was designed to suggest that many well-placed people had an interest in the future of Chile. Before the end of 1818 the exigent funds that the Chilean government could afford to send him put an end to this grandiose scheme. In 1819 he was relegated to life in a boarding house. Perhaps knowledge that other American representatives had similar schemes and already had ended up in debtors' prison induced him to take these economies. At any rate, his first diplomatic efforts were not very successful. In fact, recognition by the major powers was granted only by the United States during O'Higgins' tenure in office. Toward the end of July 1819, Irisarri reported that so long as British government officials remained ignorant of Chile and its laws there was little hope of recognition.[23] He therefore focused his attention on Lord Castlereagh, hoping to convince the Prime Minister of the advantageous nature of recognition to all concerned. But he was forced to do this indirectly, since Castlereagh continually refused to meet with the Chilean Plenipotentiary, an act which some, no doubt, would construe as being tantamount to recognition.

But by the end of August, the British government had decided to maintain a policy of strict neutrality in the Latin American wars. Now the Prime Minister could greet the Plenipotentiary officially without offending anyone. Irisarri had a diplomatic weapon whose potential value he may not have correctly gauged. In April, O'Higgins had announced officially the blockade of the Pacific coast from Iquique in southern Chile all the way north to Guayaquil that recently had been declared by Lord Cochrane. Neutrals were permitted to trade, but not in war materiel, and their ships might not carry officials or merchants of countries subject to the King of Spain. Castlereagh agreed to a conference for August 23. Irisarri formulated a program of three points for the discussion: the naming of British consuls for Chile; the admission of the Chilean flag into ports of Great Britain and her colonies; and the reception of a Chilean consul general in Great Britain.[24] It was good that he was pleased with his carefully wrought plans and confident of good results, for his opponent was an experienced and wily negotiator. Irissari's enthusiasm was increased probably by the knowledge that he was not asking for formal recognition.

After the initial obligatory amenities, at which time Castlereagh apologized for not having received Irisarri sooner or answering his June communication, the new nation was baptized into the world of nations by an admirably adept host at such events. Chile would not be recognized, but since a policy of neutrality had been adopted, it would receive all the benefits attendant upon actual recognition. This was correct in a sense, especially a commercial sense, but incorrect in another and more important one: Formal recognition would have gone a long way toward discouraging Spain from sending future invasion forces. Then Castlereagh began to pick apart Irisarri's three points. The Chilean brought up the question of British consuls being sent to Chile, a logical step in light of the Prime Minister's thoughtful reference to the advantages of neutrality. But Castlereagh talked his way around and out of this suggestion. That took care of point one. The sending of British consuls to Chile alone may have had some appeal to Castlereagh, no doubt aware of the commercial possibilities this suggested, but the reverse was not timely. The appearance of Chilean consuls in Britain would have embarrassed the British government in its relations with Spain. And since Britain was not going to send consuls, she certainly could not receive them. So much for point three.

Now the Prime Minister took the offensive; he had some horse trading to do. He said his government considered the Chilean blockade of the entire coast of Peru illegal because the Chilean fleet did not possess enough ships to maintain it. It was a paper blockade, and Great Britain was not going to respect it. Irisarri vainly attempted to defend the blockade, but he actually knew very little about the fleet, and was not convincing. He got off the subject by asking that with neutrality established could ships flying the Chilean flag enter British ports? Castlereagh answered in the affirmative for ships of commerce. Irisarri then queried if this applied also to ships-of-war. The answer was yes if they did not bring war prizes, and if the privilege was reciprocal for Great Britain. Irisarri agreed. And on this note the conference terminated.

The Prime Minister clearly took the day. The Chilean's first and second points were disposed of with professional alacrity. Castlereagh agreed to the second point—a hollow victory at best for Irisarri, since no Chilean ship of commerce or war had yet entered a British port, and the Empire rightly did not anticipate a traffic jam produced by Chilean ships—which cost him little indeed, but in return he achieved the virtual end of the Chilean blockade. Britain maintained a fleet in the Pacific to protect her interests, especially commercial, and considered it necessary to enter the ports of countries in which her citizens resided or did business. This privilege Castlereagh now received from Irisarri. The most important result of the meeting was not even reported by Irisarri to the Chilean government. Castlereagh declared that Great Britain would not aid any European power in a war against a Latin American country. Though this attitude did not guarantee independence, it would discourage further aggression.

Irisarri understood that he had done all he could in Great Britain for the moment and wanted to proceed directly to the United States. In February 1819 the Chilean government approved an abortive loan of 3,000,000 pesos at 12 per cent from a citizen of the United States, Jeremey Robinson. O'Higgins then named him his agent to the United States, and the Senate approved at a secret session, stating that his principal object would be to arrange "the recognition of our independence. . . ." It is not certain whether Irisarri knew this. At any rate, he made the acquaintance of United States Minister Rush, who informed him that Congress was palpably disposed toward recognition. He urged Irisarri to make the trip to Washington without delay. And this Irisarri would have done save for the lack of funds. Instead, he wrote a letter soliciting recognition, but he judged it had little chance of success so long as the United States was negotiating with Spain over the Florida question. Now Irisarri settled down into the dull routine of diplomacy. His hope was to convince Europe of the desirability of recognition. To achieve this end, he became an active and articulate contributor to British newspapers and journals. But he was not always sure what he was advocating. In November 1820 he unsuccessfully challenged O'Higgins to declare the principles on which his government was framed so people in Europe would know what they would be recognizing. This "because no one knows what there is to recognize, if it is a democratic Republic, artistocratic or a monarchy or a government without principles." [25] Irisarri obviously was not one to mince words. Before he died he would earn a lasting reputation as one of the most controversial figures in Chilean history.

Though O'Higgins had decreed freedom of the press in July, the statement was not published until October. "From today there will be," the decree read, "total and absolute freedom of press." Yet as was customary a tribunal was established to insure the freedom of press and prosecute offenders. And, as one might expect, this freedom did not apply to religious writings, which remained subject to government approval. Not only were there these qualifications, but O'Higgins believed in freedom of press only to the degree that individuals, organizations, and especially the government were not slandered. This was naturally subject to much personal interpretation, and the Chilean liberals were patently notable for a low tolerance of criticism. Had the situation been less fluid they might better have lived up to their own principles.

A British traveler, Gilbert F. Mathison, described the press shortly after his visit to Chile in 1821: "In Chile, under the government of O'Higgins, it has long been declared free; yet either no one dares to take advantage of this professed liberty to deliver political opinions, or no one has the spirit and talent of a ready writer." Mathison observed that he had heard "of one unfortunate German, who, good easy man! believed to the letter all the fine things that were said by the government, of the existence and in praise of a free press, and who, to try the reality of its existence, undertook the publication of a political work. What was the consequence? His presses were seized, every copy of his work destroyed, and himself sent off by a summary process to the almost desert island of Juan Fernandez, there to keep company with other State prisoners, and mourn over his blundering credulity." [26] It is not likely that this was a unique situation.

The Supreme Director proposed the creation of a corps of military engineers late in the fall. The Senate refused to give its approval to the scheme due to the shortage of funds. And in so doing gave further evidence of the civilian nature of Chilean liberalism. However, O'Higgins did not require Senate approval on all issues. In November Protestant members of the foreign community resident in Chile sent a joint letter to him requesting permission to establish cemeteries in Santiago and Valparaíso. The foreigners, some of whom had already obtained Chilean citizenship, noted that at times Protestants on their deathbeds had converted to Catholicism merely to insure burial. Others who managed to get buried as Protestants sometimes found themselves disinterred and on the beach at Valparaíso. In December O'Higgins decreed that the Protestants could purchase land for the purpose of establishing a cemetery in Santiago and one in Valparaíso. This may appear less courageous than it was. Such an unprecedented provocative decision certainly would agitate supporters and enemies alike.

Two other senatorial decisions during the year 1819 deserve special attention. In June of the previous year the Supreme Director decreed the abolition of the *mayorazgos.* This institution by which a property owner, in theory not necessarily of land, could pass his estate intact along to his first born, was the sinew which kept the Chilean aristocracy in place. This does not exclude the non-titled wealthy, who also guaranteed the integrity of their fortunes through the *mayorazgo.* And indeed the June measure was not popular with a citizenry partisan to a liberal tradition that placed sanctity of property rights among its cardinal principles. A legal case involving the legitimacy of a *mayorazgo* was referred by an Intendant to the Senate in 1819. In December the contentious Senate reversed O'Higgins' decree by postponing its authority "for now." The *mayorazgo* was not abolished permanently for several decades, at which time the institution was supported more vigorously by the business community than by the agrarians. One must admire O'Higgins' zeal as a reformer and lament his obtuse sense of political timing. Neither the government nor the country at large chanced to gain much in the near future by the destruction of entailed estates, but both stood to suffer from such a significant alteration in basic agricultural patterns and the alienation of the landed wealthy from the administration so prematurely.

Also in December the Senate continued to involve itself in military matters. O'Higgins was ordered to accelerate his efforts to ready the *Expedición Libertadora* for departure. Lord Cochrane's questionable successes so far had enthused the Senators to demand greater things. They ordered the Supreme Director to make his final arrangements so that when the fleet should arrive the expedition could leave without delay. The departure would take place whether or not San Martín and his Argentine troops were prepared to accompany the expedition. Not only was it enormously pretentious of the Senate to presume to know at what speed an army should be prepared for war, but its disenchantment with San Martín and the inclination to carry out the liberation of Peru without the Argentine troops bespeaks the intensity of Chilean nationalism. By the end of 1819 one can say that the Senate already had begun to represent Chilean nationhood to the Chileans, and O'Higgins the independence of Chile and an irrevocable debt to a foreign power.

During the summer and fall of 1820 both the Supreme Director and Senate devoted most of their energies to the final preparations for the *Expedición Libertadora*. In January San Martín was named General of the united armies, and orders were given to raise the number of troops to six thousand. Senatorial ardor had not abated during the heat of a Santiago summer. In February it decided that the invasion would comprise six thousand troops whether or not the United Provinces contributed to that number. Finance continued to threaten the military buildup. The government judged that it required 300,000 additional pesos to outfit the expedition. In March the Senate declared that it was useless to expect further contributions from the monasteries and clergy, since they no longer had anything to give. Instead, the Senate proposed that all foreigners who had obtained citizenship must contribute a specific amount, and those foreigners who were not citizens were requested to contribute voluntarily "in order to aid our cause." There was a substantial foreign community in Chile by now. Many had taken out Chilean citizenship for various reasons, not the least of which was that citizenship entitled them to partake of the lucrative trade reserved for nationals. The government had extended them coveted privileges and now wanted repayment. The following month further privileges were granted to foreigners by the Senate. Domestic shipping facilities were not large enough to service the entire nation satisfactorily. Northern miners consequently requested that foreigners be permitted to carry copper out of the northern regions and carry in food and commercial items. Apart from the fact that the nation's mining industry suffered from the prohibitions against foreign participation in the nation's coastal trade, the Senate could hardly refuse the miners' pleas now that foreigners were contributing financially to the cause of liberation. But in June the British merchants who were not citizens complained that in the matter of financial contributions their rights as citizens of a neutral nation were being infringed upon. They appealed to the commander of the British fleet in the Pacific, and a formal protest was lodged with the Senate. Early in July that body ruled that the complaint was totally lacking in legal principle, but in the name of harmony it rescinded the previous decision that foreigners had to contribute voluntarily to the support of the *Expedición Libertadora.* Just at the moment that the Chilean fleet was expected to sail, the government clearly did not consider itself in a position to anger Great Britain and, more importantly, the British fleet.

Several other measures were adopted to increase the national income. In May O'Higgins had appointed a special tribunal to supervise the collection of taxes. The Senate approved, and the tribunal was named in June. Finances caused the government more anxiety than any other problem during the winter months of 1820, as it hurried the preparations for the invasion force. Yet it found itself capable of raising the Supreme Director's salary. O'Higgins' income plainly was insufficient to meet his official obligations. In July the Senate raised it from eight thousand pesos annually to twelve thousand. And in September, just after the *Expedición Libertadora* sailed, the Senate granted him outright eight thousand pesos to pay his personal debts. O'Higgins was scrupulously honest, and being Supreme Director meant no financial advantage to him at least.

While the government was concentrating its efforts on preparing the invasion force, O'Higgins was particularly interested in securing recognition from foreign powers. Properly timed, recognition would have stimulated morale and lent a note of international blessing to the liberation effort. Thus, O'Higgins was especially chagrined to read in newspapers printed in Buenos Aires that the Chilean government supported plans to establish a monarchy in the South American continent. In an April letter to John B. Prevost, then in Buenos Aires, he attempted to dispel such rumors: "My surprise was great . . . and never until I see it, can I believe that Mr. Irisarri has forfeited his character and contravened my instructions by lending his ear to such a proposal —You are convinced I hope of my republican sentiments and I can assure you that I would rather die, than to stain my name with such a dereliction of my Duty and of my principles." This letter is sometimes cited to demonstrate O'Higgins' fervent republicanism. However, it was a diplomatic note and as such cannot be taken too literally. O'Higgins manifested a sure sense for international diplomacy, as this letter further suggests.

For the ultimate preparations concerning the *Expedición Libertadora,* O'Higgins went to Valparaíso personally. At seven in the evening of August 20 he wrote that at that moment the fleet was weighing anchor. That moment took much longer to arrive than had been envisaged while the Army of the Andes was taking shape on the other side of the cordillera, and it affected the lives of O'Higgins and San Martín in ways that probably they never perceived that long ago. The public careers of both men were fast drawing to a close.

CHAPTER VI

The Second Phase of Government

JUST DAYS AFTER THE FLEET SAILED IN AUGUST 1820, THE SENATE created two positions of captain general and named O'Higgins to one of them. So great was the Senate's enthusiasm that it made the positions retroactive to 1818 when O'Higgins himself had abolished the position of great marshal. But it was not long until the Senate and Supreme Director came into conflict once again. In late June the Senate had written and approved the instructions that were designed to govern San Martín's activities in Peru. O'Higgins was asked to make observations, but it was not suggested that he could alter them. The instructions ordered the General-in-Chief to grant Peru a new constitution, one which, it is not surprising, would not alter the status of slaves. Force would be applied only where absolutely necessary. San Martín was told to be careful of appropriate conduct; there would be no plunder or confiscation of property except when he was sure that those involved were royalists. Certainly, these instructions presumed upon the military authority of the Supreme Director.

But the Senators went even further: They suggested that the government send a diplomatic deputy to Peru and even suggested a list of three from which the choice should be made. This was a direct encroachment on the Supreme Director's political authority. O'Higgins responded by refusing to pass the instructions along to San Martín. Rather, he granted the General-in-Chief blanket powers. The Senate received O'Higgins' excuses late in September. The Supreme Director catalogued San Martín's virtues and concluded that the instructions would threaten morale. In early October the Senate declared that O'Higgins' reasons were unsatisfactory and insisted that the instructions be communicated to San Martín. The Senators agreed that San Martín should have total military freedom, but, they believed, the type of government to be created in Peru must be decided in Chile. O'Higgins did not send the instructions.

Yet this was not the only point of dispute. In the spring of 1820 the Minister of War informed the Senate that enemies of the state had wrought considerable damage in the province of Concepción and requested that permission be granted the Supreme Director to send troops and materiel by land and sea to the south. This the Senate did. Now a war was being fought both at home and abroad. It was under these circumstances that O'Higgins proposed salary increases for certain military officers. The Senate refused to approve the proposal. Clearly the Supreme Director was something less than a strong dictator. In December the Senate abrogated all wartime extraordinary powers that had been granted to O'Higgins.

Captain Samuel Hill of the United States merchant ships "Ophelia" and "Packet" visited Chile twice during the period 1815 to 1822 and was not always impressed with what he witnessed. In his journal, he recorded for the date October 1820: "No permanent System of Finance had yet been established whereby the Expenses of the Government & of the War might be defrayed, and on every emergency Recourse was had to temporary loans & forced Contributions. Nothing like a regular appraisement of Lands & other Permanent Property had yet been attempted, or any one Species of Regular Taxation resorted to, and when arbitrary contributions were levied the quotas were evidently determined by favouritism or Caprice." Hill also commented on public morality: "The Publick officers of the Chilean State Government are Said to be exceedingly Corrupt, & profligate of the Public money. Gambling to an enormous amount is encouraged & practised by all Classes & indeed it is the established Custom of the Country, it is evidently productive of many disorders & Vices of Serious Magnitude." Probably without intending it, Hill thus gave a vote of confidence to O'Higgins' public morality decrees. He was indeed a harsh critic. There appears to be some confusion of dates in his journal, but the following observation seems to have been meant also for 1820: "In short the Government at present is a Military Tyranny in the Strictest acceptation of the Term—And the People long accustomed to Slavery, See more to please, than to be displeased with, and find Consolation in the reflection that their present Self elected Masters are of their own Sail, & not of foreign Growth." [1] Actually, he was incorrect on both accounts.

Domestic activities during 1821 were not unusual. On the international front all attention remained focused on the outcome of the expedition to Peru. The liberation effort now stretched the financial imagination of government officials beyond endurance.

Plans were drawn to strengthen the currency through the creation of a bank that was not soon to materialize. Still, in 1820 the Senate had resolved to re-establish the colonial tobacco monopoly, called the *estanco*. It was hoped that the *estanco* would succor the public treasury. The actual decree as signed by O'Higgins was not published until April 1821. It prohibited the free commerce in foreign tobacco. Coincident with this and related restrictions placed on the economy by the government was O'Higgins' accelerated campaign to obtain United States recognition. In January Prevost informed Adams that the Supreme Director had insured him that a republican form of government would be adopted by Chile when the provisional government ceased to exist. But it was for this reason that O'Higgins desired "an early recognition on our part—He is persuaded that it would set the matter at rest, and that our political institutions would become the model from which those of South America would be formed." Once again O'Higgins demonstrated his sensitive diplomatic acumen. Prevost warmly admired O'Higgins' political sentiments: "He is truly a republican Patriot and in heart opposed to everything in the shape of Monarchy and will resist its adoption although assurances have been made through his agents in Europe of an acknowledgement of Chile when he shall consent to establish that form of Government." It was perhaps his interest in recognition that induced O'Higgins to accept the protests of the merchant community against the *estanco*. In May he decreed its suspension for two years. But still recognition was not granted.

Meanwhile, the *Expedición Libertadora* was not faring well. San Martín captured the port of Pisco, to the south of Lima, and Cochrane was blockading Callao, but so far no general uprising in support of the forces of liberation materialized, as San Martín calculated would occur. Then the Argentine moved his army to a position north of Lima. Again he expected the Peruvians to share his enthusiasm for liberation and rise up against the Viceroy. While his officers, especially some of those not under his direct supervision, like Cochrane, grew restless through the lack of resolution and action, San Martín entered into fruitless negotiations with Viceroy Pezuela. Both seemed determined to avoid an ultimate confrontation. Eventually, San Martín elected to march toward Lima, and, as he approached, the royalist army deposed Pezuela and selected a new Viceroy, one who withdrew in a short while owing to Lima's low food supply, not out of military weakness. On July 10 the army of the *Expedición Libertadora* entered

Lima in passive triumph. It is quite fashionable to refer to San Martín as a military genius. Certain it is that he demonstrated a notable degree of ability, but he was hardly a military genius. He was a trained militarist among civilians-turned-soldiers and conspicuously few professionals. No doubt he evinced excellence as an organizer and planner of campaigns, but in the field he rarely won—or deserved—the accolades of the professionals whom he led.

The independence of Peru was quickly proclaimed, and San Martín became the chief of state with the title *Protector*. To this news O'Higgins responded with lively praise. But the Supreme Director was despondent over his relations with the Senate, which had blocked his every attempt to supply the forces in Peru and even in southern Chile. The Senate had lowered duties on selected items and ended the monthly tax contribution. And this at a time when guerrilla troops were enjoying a restoration in the south. In early August O'Higgins lamented to San Martín that he was faced with the choice of dissolving the Senate or losing the province of Concepción. Most perplexing was the fact that the Senators were hand-picked and supposedly friends. O'Higgins pondered the unpleasant conclusion: "what will those who are indifferent and elected by the unbridled multitude do?" He urged San Martín to profit from this experience.

Though the Supreme Director and Senate obviously were not on the best of terms, they both managed to proceed with the ordinary business of administering the country. In mid-July O'Higgins decreed that the constitutional clause declaring the children born to slaves to be free must be observed strictly. In August the *Gaceta Ministerial* noted that Diego Thomson soon would arrive in Santiago to establish a school based on the Lancaster system of mutual instruction. The editorial which made this announcement public was a credit to the liberal credo. It observed that ignorance was one of the greatest evils man could suffer; it was the origin of a great part of his errors and miseries, and the key to tyranny. Education was certainly a central goal of the Chilean liberals. The country required, the editor noted, "a liberty regulated by laws, customs and opinions. . . . No one can be happy if he does not study his Religion, his morality, his rights, if he does not take advantage of the knowledge of those who preceded him. . . ." The school opened on September 18, just eleven years after the first Junta was established.

While the Supreme Director and Senate proceeded working together in an uneasy harmony, producing scores of laws relating to all aspects of society, a conflict between the Protector and Admiral Cochrane threatened to vitiate the Peruvian success. San Martín's caution and lack of initiative in the months preceding the entrance into Lima thoroughly tortured the impulsive naval hero. Once San Martín became Protector, Cochrane requested that the fleet be paid its back salaries. San Martín replied that his government was responsible only for the prizes taken since the campaign commenced and that the fleet salaries were to be paid by Chile. In knowledge of the debilitating sacrifices made by Chile to mount the invasion in the first place, Cochrane considered San Martín's position untenable and unjust.

In early September the Protector sent a sizable amount of money to the port of Ancón, and the Admiral seized it. However, he did sign for the money. The real damage occurred when he directly disobeyed San Martín's orders by paying off the fleet. As a result of the argument which followed, Cochrane took his fleet out of Peruvian waters and searched out Spanish ships all the way to Mexico, returning to Chile in the middle of 1822. In a "Most secret and confidential" letter to his "Dear Friend Lord Cochrane," O'Higgins wrote in English: *"I would have done the same if I had been there, therefore I say again all has my approbation. . . ."* O'Higgins referred to the affair at Ancón. Yet this contretemps did not disrupt the liberation effort. At Callao alone San Martín recovered eight hundred cannons of various sizes, and as he reported to O'Higgins the only army which could sustain a royalist effort was disorganized and incapable of such a major feat. "Peru is free. . . ." [2]

It is clear that O'Higgins vacillated between monarchism and republicanism in his first two years as Supreme Director. But in October 1821 he wrote two letters that indicate he now made a decision in favor of republicanism. Both letters were to friends, and to neither did he have to write in guarded platitudes. In the first he wrote that "if our sacrifices have not had an insignificant object; if the creators of the revolution resolved to make their world free and happy and this is achieved only under a Republican Government and not through the variation of distant dynasties; it is necessary that we escape those cold calculators who crave monarchism. . . ." In this letter he alluded to the physical nature of Chile. In the second, he expanded on this theme, observing, "It is necessary to see the tendency of the population, its physical, moral and political state," in order to select a government. Again he advocated republicanism. He observed that

Chile's revolution should produce more than merely a "nominal change in dynasty."

Two additional domestic matters in 1821 deserve special attention. In the fall of the year the famous Maipo Canal was completed. Started during the colonial period, work on the project received little government support between 1810 and 1818. But O'Higgins took up its cause and deserves credit for the final result. Located just outside Santiago, the canal promised to stimulate agricultural productivity in the central region, and this it eventually did. It was the one major internal improvement of the O'Higgins administration. During the same year, a United States citizen, Daniel S. Grisnold, presented the government a solicitation requesting a concession of a fifteen-year exclusive privilege for the establishment of steam navigation in Chilean waters. Both O'Higgins and Minister Zenteno supported the solicitation, but other officials opposed it. Finally in the middle of March a concession was granted, but it allowed only a ten-year exclusive privilege. For some reason the franchise never was implemented. During the following year two steam vessels worked in Chilean waters, but their success was short-lived. It remained for a North American, William Wheelwright, to establish an effective steam service in Chile in 1840.

The year 1822 was O'Higgins' last full year in office. Considering the vexatious moments he was destined to live, it was probably a good thing that he had determined his own convictions. Even as early as January it should have been certain that it would be a tumultuous year for the Chilean government. O'Higgins desired the support of the Church, but he was jealous of his prerogatives as Supreme Director. In 1821 he and the Senate made arrangements to send José Ignacio Cienfuegos to the Vatican to reach an accord. The Chileans did not know that in 1816 the Pope had circulated an encyclical which supported the system of Ferdinand VII and called for an end to the independence movement. The encyclical was published in Spanish in Lima in 1820, and members of the *Expedición Libertadora* were the first Chileans to see it. It is reported that when San Martín saw the encyclical he said that it was too bad there were not two or three thousand of them, since the army needed paper for munitions.[3] At any rate, it was under such inauspicious circumstances that Cienfuegos left for Rome in January 1822. It just so happens that he was also one of Chile's five Senators. A second Senator was sent as the Chilean representative to the new government in Peru.

That left the country with only three Senators, with one more hoping to return to private life. And this proved extremely tempting to the Supreme Director.

Thus, in January O'Higgins suggested that since so few Senators were available for actual legislative work, the Senate should temporarily suspend its sessions. He proposed that the senatorial duties be transferred to the Supreme Director, who would be responsible for his actions to the Senate once it commenced to meet again. Whatever else may have displeased various factions, whatever else he had done in the past that ended by dislodging sections of his own support from under himself, nothing was quite so impressive as this political indiscretion. And the timing was just perfect. O'Higgins was alone now; the south was fairly quiet; the leader of the guerrillas, Benavides, was soon to be executed; and Peru was on the way to liberation. It was time for the Supreme Director to leave public life, all conceivable goals of the independence movement, except perhaps a permanent constitution, having been achieved, or give the government an entirely Chilean character, Chile's first truly national government. And this he probably would have been able to accomplish if only his training as a political ideologist had been concerned with peace rather than war, if only he had better understood the political nature of the active Chilean citizenry.

The degree to which he was untutored in such matters is evident in his subornation of the Senate. His leading supporters clearly were liberals, and it appears that a vast number of active citizens, though they may not have been political theorists, had a predilection for liberalism. Theirs was in many ways a conservative theory of government, but that, after all, was the nature of classical liberalism, especially when juxtaposed to the more radical theory of democracy. O'Higgins may well have disaffected fewer supporters had he suggested the establishment of a monarchy rather than the suspension of the Senate. More than an elected Supreme Director or a President, the Senate was designed to be the guardian of the canons of liberalism, and in the Chilean case the Senate more than the Supreme Director represented the maturing national character. It was fortunate for O'Higgins that there were still many loose ends to be tied together: The liberation effort in Peru had to be supported; the south had to be rehabilitated after so many years of warfare; and the United Provinces presented a fearsome spectacle of instability. In calmer times his attempt to usurp the legislative functions of government might have led to an earlier retirement from public life than actually occurred.

The recalcitrant Senate refused to be abused. In early February 1822 it replied to the Supreme Director's proposal with a vigorous statement declaring that it did not consider itself authorized to suspend sessions, and less authorized to give its own authority to the Supreme Director. The unconstitutionality of such an act was stressed. The Senate must exist, it argued, to guard over the constitution, for without the Senate there is no constitution. If the Senate were no longer necessary, then a Congress should be convened to which it would turn over its powers. Diego Barros Arana claims that the Senate itself had suggested it suspend sessions in May of 1821. This was certainly precedent for O'Higgins, but the circumstances were very different then: Theoretically, Chile was still in a state of war, and at such times power traditionally was transferred to one individual. That the Senate reversed its position, and in so doing depriving its answer to O'Higgins' proposal of some dignity, was due to the altered conditions of 1822 and a fear that dissolution of the Senate would concentrate too much power in the hands of the powerful Minister José Antonio Rodríguez Aldea.

By 1822 Rodríguez Aldea was O'Higgins' most influential minister, one who became less popular with each month in office. His rise to power reflects several fundamental characteristics of the O'Higgins regime. Born in Chillán in 1779, he began practicing law at the turn of the century, and was in Peru as notary to the ecclesiastical tribunal when the independence movement got under way. He returned to his homeland as military legal adviser to the army led by General Gaínza. He and O'Higgins met during the negotiations that resulted in the Treaty of Lircay, each representing an opposite side. During the reconquest, after the defeat at Rancagua, he continued on in Santiago as the royalist army's legal adviser. After the patriot success at Chacabuco he retired to private life, but when Osorio landed at Talcahuano he was ordered to leave Chile. However, O'Higgins had established a very lenient policy toward royalists who desired to pledge themselves to the patriot cause. This he did and consequently was permitted to remain in Santiago. In early 1820 O'Higgins named him Minister of Treasury. In the succeeding years, at a time when the Supreme Director's clement policy toward former royalists became even more conciliatory, Rodríguez Aldea became O'Higgins' most trusted counselor and easily the most powerful figure in government next to his one superior. His is an illustrative example both of the government's policy toward former royalists and the degree to which there were trained bureaucrats available to staff administrative posts. There were not many, but there were enough to provide for professional administration. The scarcity of trained personnel has been much overstated. In addition, Rodríguez Aldea's background suggests something that often is forgotten about the independence movement: There were dedicated Chileans, loyal Chileans, on the losing side also.

While O'Higgins and the Senate were bringing their aging conflicts to perhaps a logical conclusion, Irisarri was still in London imploring his government to join with the other important nations of Latin America in establishing some kind of uniform political outlook. Irisarri believed this the only means by which recognition could be secured.[4] In May he was convinced that the government of the United States would recommend to Congress the recognition of the Latin American nations. That government, he observed, appreciated the commercial advantages enjoyed by Great Britain, though gained without recognition, and understood that recognition would eliminate the invidious gap.[5] As it turned out Irisarri's premonitory note proved correct, but one would not suspect it from a message sent by United States Commercial Agent at Valparaíso, Michael Hogan, just a few days earlier. To Adams Hogan charged: "The course this government has pursued for some months past appears calculated to annihilate commerce, they expect to obtain an acknowledgement of their Independence by coercion. . . ." Though recognition was extended by the United States during the same year, Irisarri gave up hope of an immediate recognition from Great Britain and before the end of the year transferred his energies to France, which traditionally had sided with Spain.

Prior to the convocation in May of a convention to write a permanent constitution, the Senate and Supreme Director were to have one last important fight. The provisional Constitution of 1818 stipulated that intendants and governors must be selected by popular election. Owing to the unsettled conditions during the year 1821, the Senate ruled that the Supreme Director could appoint the governors of Valparaíso, Talcahuano, and Valdivia, and the intendant of Concepción. During the relatively tranquil months of 1822 the Senate demanded that the Supreme Director provide for elections of all governors and intendants. As usual it was the Senate that guarded the presumptions of liberalism. Whatever harmony had existed between the Senate and Supreme

Director had by now dissipated into frigid hostility. Moreover, there was considerable pressure for the calling of a constitutional convention. Camilo Henríquez argued that it was now time to carry the program of the independence movement to fruition. Minister Rodríguez Aldea surveyed the various sentiments and concluded that this was an advantageous moment, one which would allow the creation of an even stronger executive. For O'Higgins, Henríquez was too radical and Rodríguez Aldea too conservative.

The Supreme Director signed the decree on May 7 that convoked the convention to prepare a constitution. It stated that any citizen over twenty-five years of age could be elected a delegate if he possessed some immovable or industrial property. The delegates would receive no remuneration. The election would be carried out by municipalities. There are no better circumstances under which one can judge accurately the political theories of Latin American statesmen than those created by elections. What they say in speeches or diplomatic correspondence is one thing; what they do at election time is what counts. O'Higgins sent delegates to the provinces to preside over the elections. Notes were sent to the important provincial officials actually stipulating who should be elected. Thus, on the same day that he signed the convocation decree, O'Higgins wrote to Ramón Freire, Intendant of Concepción, naming the individual to be elected. That O'Higgins was a classical liberal is certain from his various actions as Supreme Director; that his brand of liberalism was not often compatible with democracy, was indeed of the conservative variety, is also sure. O'Higgins sent out many notes, but asked that only a few be returned to him. This was most impolitic. Freire, for instance, was ordered to make the nomination of Santiago Fernandez immediately and indicate at the bottom of O'Higgins' letter that this was accomplished. Then the letter was to be returned at once to the capital. Not only did this procedure indicate that O'Higgins considered it necessary to check on Freire's compliance with the order, but worse, it suggested that O'Higgins did not trust Freire with the letter itself. This was no little slight. Freire led the revolution that soon ousted O'Higgins from power.

The Convention met for the first time on July 23, 1822. O'Higgins addressed the delegates and announced that his term of office had now terminated. The delegates refused to accept his resignation. O'Higgins replied that by so doing the Convention approved his past official actions. It was awkward logic, and considering the manner in which the delegates were elected one must question O'Higgins' sincerity. Through this dubious gesture he earned himself a spurious mandate. In his opening speech the Supreme Director observed candidly that the Convention did not represent the entire nation, at least to the degree that would have been the case in some other countries, and to the degree that would be the case some day in Chile also, but it was a "respectable popular election, and the only one that legally one could have for now. . . ." O'Higgins told the delegates that his desire had always been the establishment in Chile of "a representative government, whatever be its denomination. . . ." But, he noted, general opinion supported by reason and experience commanded that the supreme executive power be invested in a single magistrate, who would work within certain institutional checks. Surely he was talking about a strong executive, for he stressed the importance of the checks: without them "vacillates authority, security, and all the foundations of society and of prosperity are disturbed and annulled." The evidence indicates that O'Higgins genuinely believed this. There was no ideological paradox between this admirable sentiment and his perversion of the electoral process. His was a provisional, indeed a revolutionary government, and even a radical French democrat would have understood and perhaps applauded the construction of a stable government at the expense of certain principles that would have greater validity in more tranquil times. The trouble is that many Chileans had come to believe that such times had arrived. And once a significant number of influential Chileans thought this to be true, O'Higgins' personal limitations as an ideologist and political leader rendered him a burdensome anachronism.

Once the Convention convened the Senate dissolved itself, and the Convention assumed legislative power. One could argue that this was more or less what the framers of the Constitution of 1818 had in mind when they provided for a Senate that would turn over its powers to a Congress when one should be called into existence. At any rate, the Convention now furnished O'Higgins' regime an additional aura of respectability. And it proved to be quite amenable to the Supreme Director's wishes. This respectability the government needed because a major scandal was in the making. It was fairly well-known that Minister Rodríguez Aldea and a merchant, Antonio Arcos, had joined forces and were speculating in commodities, especially tobacco. By cornering the market in a commodity and then raising import duties, the two artificially inflated profits and their fortunes. Though no one seems to have suspected O'Higgins of collusion, for his personal reputation was impeccable, it was rumored that his sister was Minister Rodríguez Aldea's partner.

During July and August these financial improprieties merely served to instigate discontent, most notably in commercial circles. Unfortunately, O'Higgins was now faced with other serious problems. The worst was with the Church. Late in 1821 the wife of one of the nation's leading revolutionary leaders, an important citizen, and soon to be President of Chile, Joaquín Prieto, was asked to leave church services because of the manner in which she was dressed. A conflict over the matter arose between the Supreme Director and a clergyman, José Alejo Eyzaguirre. O'Higgins actually incarcerated the priest, who quickly complained that his rights under canon law had been violated. O'Higgins responded by exiling him for one year to Mendoza. However incorrect the priest may have been for confronting the Supreme Director, O'Higgins' actions were inexcusable. The whole affair became somewhat of a public matter, and O'Higgins' standing with the Church suffered another severe jolt. His patronization of a public theater in Santiago further appalled Church leaders. During the winter of 1822 a friend had written from across the cordillera that travelers informed him of considerable public discontent with the Chilean ministers and the administration itself. O'Higgins answered that he was aware of this discontent, but he defended the expulsion of Eyzaguirre, thus acknowledging the importance of the Church in the general malcontent.

Just about a week after he defended his position in the Eyzaguirre affair, the Supreme Director made one of the most momentous decrees of his entire administration. On August 21 he permitted Bishop Rodríguez to return from Mendoza to assume his former position with full powers. Exiled for several years, the Bishop indeed was pleased to return to Chile, and as an indication of this shortly made a patriotic statement. Judged alone, this act of restoring the nation's leading ecclesiastical official to his position and powers might well have enhanced O'Higgins' own public image. But coupled with his actions during the month of September it took on an element of contrition and suggested that the Supreme Director sought the favor of royalist elements. With the Convention as his legislature, and while both awaited the draft of a constitution, O'Higgins promulgated laws that induced many supporters to question his loyalty. Specifically, a general amnesty was declared for all royalists, except for those convicted of murder or military revolt. All prisoners of war would be freed when Spain recognized the independence of the nation. On the surface, this might have been received merely as a magnanimous gesture, a measure of the new nation's stability and confidence. But there was more: O'Higgins also decreed that since royalists were now restored to their full political rights as Chileans, their expropriated real property must be returned. Though this does not seem to have pertained to royalists living abroad, it was more than many a good patriot could stand, whether or not his indignation was inspired by this threat to an economic position acquired at the expense of the royalists. It probably became a not uncommon thing to question the Supreme Director's patriotism.

Late in August, just as O'Higgins' regime was developing its terminal pains, María Graham, a trained artist and wife of a British naval officer who died on the trip which recently brought Mrs. Graham to Chile, recorded one of the most sensitive and revealing personal observations ever made about the Supreme Director. O'Higgins knew relatives of Mrs. Graham's in England and was happy to receive her at the directorial palace. "He is modest and simple, and plain in his manners, arrogating nothing to himself; or, if he has done much, ascribing it to the influence of that love of country which, as he says, may inspire great feelings into an ordinary man." O'Higgins was sure that his visitor must have been surprised at the backwardness of the country in many things. He "particularly mentioned the want of religious toleration, or, rather, the very small measure of it which, considering the general state of things, he had yet been able to grant, without disturbing the public tranquility. . . ." The question of religious toleration placed O'Higgins in one of those enervating predicaments that now were becoming exasperatingly familiar. On the one hand, his inclination to encourage foreign immigration and his willingness to relax religious restrictions alienated the Church and many of his more conservative followers; on the other, the foreigners and some of the more radical Chileans wanted greater religious freedom. O'Higgins "seemed a little inclined to censure those Protestants who wished prematurely to force upon him the building of a chapel, and the public institution of Protestant worship; forgetting how very short time it is since even private liberty of conscience and a consecrated burial-place had been allowed in a country which, within twelve years, had been subject to the Inquisition at Lima." There was also the artist's physical observations: "The Director was dressed, as I believe he always is, in his general's uniform; he is short and fat, yet very active: his blue eyes, light hair, and ruddy and rather coarse complexion, do not bely his Irish extraction; while his very small and short hands and feet belong to his Araucanian pedigree." [6]

In October Chile adopted a constitution designed to be permanent, but which lasted only about a year. Had he maintained the perspective that had persuaded him to become a revolutionary now so long ago, O'Higgins would have made October his last month in office. This would have been a happy choice.

CHAPTER VII

The Prolongation of Power

BY THE FIRST OF OCTOBER THE CHILEAN FLEET HAD BEEN ANCHORED at Valparaíso for some time, a period of relative inactivity during which personnel were not being paid. Back at the port from her visit to the capital, María Graham recorded the unhealthy situation in her journal under the dateline October 1, 1822: "I find that the affairs of the government are much worse than when I left the port: the wages are yet unpaid, and the crews of the ships are becoming clamorous for money, for clothing, and all other necessities. Discontent is spreading wide, and, as usual, directed against every object and every person, with or without reason." [1] But there was also considerable civil protest, especially in the nation's chief port. The insidious activities of Minister of Treasury Rodríguez Aldea and the merchant Arcos had long provoked the commercial community, but now it was rumored that they had increased their efforts and were going to reap greater profits through new legislation that would favor their carefully engineered positions.

So great was the perverse influence of Rodríguez Aldea that to be generous one must conclude that by the end of winter 1822 the administration of Chile had become a complicated and sophisticated matter, and that by then O'Higgins was being overwhelmed by questions which were beyond his reach. While he was concentrating on such pressing business as a constitution and the fleet, far more subtle matters were being worked out by Rodríguez Aldea. One of these was the question of the general benefit to be derived by the exportation of wheat and other grains from the province of Concepción, especially since such traffic would compete with the staples the Minister was exporting from Valparaíso. Thus, a decree was passed which prohibited the exportation of these products from the province of Concepción. For this restriction Intendant Freire was reproved publicly. In an attempt to protect his own reputation Freire wrote to O'Higgins informing him that the prohibition was not of his own making, but, rather, was the result of a decree promulgated by Minister Rodríguez

Aldea. Unwittingly, Freire had insulted the Supreme Director. O'Higgins replied caustically that he, not Rodríguez Aldea, had authored the decree. "Be assured," the Supreme Director reprimanded, "that my decrees are not the work of the ministers, since I am the one who commands in Chile and not they." This was an honorable posture for the Supreme Director to assume, but the evidence indicates that, on matters of economics at least, his fund of formal and practical education was fast becoming bankrupt, and that on such questions he was being maneuvered. It should not have been difficult for a lawyer and experienced bureaucrat like Rodríguez Aldea to lead in one direction or another a superior who trusted him and who was occupied with seemingly more important questions.

In late September and early October rumors that the government was preparing a new law controlling commerce, which involved the application of new restrictions, inspired greater unrest in the capital and provinces. Mrs. Graham described the rumor in her journal: "I have been almost overwhelmed with details about the new regulations of trade, the taxes to be laid on, and the monopolies of the minister Rodríguez. . . . In addition to the spirits and tobaccos they long ago purchased with the government money, they have now bought up the cottons, cloths, and other articles of clothing, and only their own agents . . . are able to procure such for any customer." How accurate this indictment is one cannot tell, but its real importance is that it reflected general opinion in Valparaíso.

Now the fleet and commercial community were both at odds with the government. In this volatile atmosphere the draft of the trade ordinance was presented to the Convention by Rodríguez Aldea. The hundreds of articles mostly applied restrictions and increased duties. Though the Convention threw out twenty-three articles, the Minister's intent was not extirpated. Actually, the ordinance merely confirmed positions already taken, even though it was stipulated that the new regulations would not take effect for six months. Again Graham: "I hear that it is so inconsistent, that it will defeat its own purpose." At the end of October, when she probably had time to see the ordinance, she noted that "I understand not much of these things; but there are passages so opposite to common sense, that a child must be struck with them." The ordinance declared Valparaíso the only free port, but permitted foreigners to stop at three others. This seemed unjust to Mrs. Graham, who was decidedly in favor of free trade, but it was a means of controlling noxious contraband.

Conditions clearly were uncertain and transitory by the second week of October. Additional complications arose when San Martín arrived at Valparaíso toward the end of the second week unannounced. On the thirteenth María Graham recorded: "Every one has been electrified to-day by the sudden arrival of General San Martín, the Protector of Peru, in this port." And well they might have been, for if anyone was searching for an alternative to O'Higgins here was a likely choice. San Martín's departure from Peru never has been fully explained and remains a controversial issue. While at Guayaquil to meet with Simón Bolívar, his most influential minister, Monteagudo, was expelled from office in Lima, a popularly acclaimed event. Perhaps the Protector thought he might be next.

To justify the unexpected decision, San Martín gave out that his rheumatism required that he take a cure at the baths of Cauquenes in Chile. And indeed, his failing health was usually a subject of O'Higgins' letters to the Protector. But it was rumored that he had sequestered an impressing amount of treasure aboard a ship for just such a moment. On the fourteenth Graham observed: "Reports arrive this morning that San Martín has been arrested; and that having endeavored to smuggle a quantity of gold, it is seized." Later in the same day she added: "So far from San Martín being arrested, two of the Director's aides-de-camp have arrived to pay him compliments,—besides the fort saluted his flag."

Now officially received, no matter what motivated his appearance, and O'Higgins it should be noted always chose to think the better of a man, San Martín relaxed in the port for a while before proceeding on to the baths. On October 15 he was brought to Mrs. Graham's house for tea. Her description of him is one of the most lucid and perceptive we have: He was "a very tall fine-looking man, dressed in plain black clothes. . . ." Physically, it was a highly complimentary picture: "San Martín's eye has a peculiarity in it that I never saw before but once. . . . It is dark and fine, but restless; it never seemed to fix for a moment, but that moment expressed everything. His countenance is decidedly handsome, sparkling, and intelligent; but *not open*. His manner of speaking is quick, but often obscure, with a few tricks and bywords; but a great flow of language, and a readiness to talk on all subjects."

Intellectually, it was indeed another matter. Probably no leader of Latin American independence suffered more incisive criticism by a highly literate, cosmopolitan observer: "We spoke of government; and there I think his ideas are far from being either clear or decisive. . . . He has not read much, nor is his genius of that stamp that can go alone. Accordingly, he continually quoted authors whom he evidently knew but by halves, and of the half he knew he appeared to me to mistake the spirit." One might recall that Mrs. Graham was endeared to her countryman, Lord Cochrane, now a staunch enemy of the Protector. "Upon the whole, the visit of this evening has not impressed me much in favor of San Martín. His views are narrow, and I think selfish. His philosophy, as he calls it, and his religion, are upon a par; both are too openly used as mere masks to impose on the world; and, indeed, they are so worn as that they would not impose on any people but those he has unhappily had to rule. . . ." Though she considered him lacking in genius, she conceded that he possessed the practical talent of being able to use what he had to the fullest extent. "His fine person, his air of superiority, and that suavity of manner which has so long enabled him to lead others, give him very decided advantages." And then a perhaps not unlikely conclusion by an Englishwoman of her class and learning: "He understands English, and speaks French tolerably; and I know no person with whom it might be pleasanter to pass half an hour: but the want of heart; and the want of candour, which are evident even in conversation of any length, would never do for intimacy, far less for friendship."

But the most important event of a month crowded with auspicious happenings was the signing of the new constitution, to which O'Higgins swore allegiance on October 30.[2] Minister Rodríguez Aldea generally is given credit for preparing the draft of the document. While it would require a specialized study in itself to determine accurately the Supreme Director's role in conceiving and promulgating the constitution, it seems safe to conclude that probably he was aware of the nature of the draft and the revisions as they took place, and that certainly he found the final document satisfactory.

The general characteristics of the government were described in the early sections. The Chilean nation was said to comprise all Chileans, and the government was declared free of the Spanish monarchy or any foreign power. The document provided all the familiar personal guarantees: All Chileans were equal before the law, and in consequence, all were required to contribute toward the costs of government according to their means. On the surface, citizenship was rather inclusive. Citizens were those born in Chile and married, or at least twenty-five years old, or those who were married to a Chilean and could prove three years of residence in the country. But to be a citizen one had to be able to read and write. This last was not so restrictive as it might appear, and, in fact, was an expected manifestation of the liberal ideology that runs throughout the document. The reading and writing requirement was designed not to apply until 1833. That is, a ten-year period of grace was extended to those who as yet could not read and write. But also quite typical of the liberal thought of the day was the easy manner in which one might lose his citizenship. For instance, anyone employed as a domestic servant, or who did not have a known way of supporting himself, or who was in debt to the public treasury, would be deprived of his citizenship so long as any of these conditions prevailed. The religion of the nation was declared to be Roman Catholic, with the exclusion of any other.

The government was republican and representative. The three familiar branches were established, with the legislature being bicameral, comprising a Chamber of Deputies and a Court of Representatives. To be elected Deputy one had to be a citizen and possess property with a value of not less than two thousand pesos. The Chamber was granted broad powers, indeed, in this respect was similar to the Congress of the United States. Among its more interesting privileges were the rights to regulate commerce, approve treaties, declare war, approve the administration's budget, present a plan for general public education—a justification of the reading and writing requirements for the franchise—and protect the liberty of the press. All its bills could be vetoed by the Supreme Director, but only within fifteen days of receiving them. After that period the bills automatically would become law. Bills could be passed over the Supreme Director's veto. The Chamber of Deputies was clearly the more powerful of the two legislative houses.

The Court of Representatives was a permanent body of seven members elected by the Chamber. At least four had to be Deputies. While the Chamber was in session, the Court became a Senate and was devised to complement the legislative activities of the Chamber, but when it was not in session the Court of Representatives was charged with guarding over the constitution. At such times it could approve or create provisional legislation, and in extraordinary times convoke the Chamber into session. As liberals the framers of the constitution were particularly concerned with protecting constitutional freedoms, and the Court, though it may have smacked of reaction to a democrat, was an appropriate instrument to guarantee them while the Chamber was not in session. The legislature already had established a proprietary primacy in government during the O'Higgins years, and now was merely writing this reality into law.

The degree to which the Chileans were not influenced by the United States example is perhaps best illustrated in the nature of the Cabinet. It was composed of ministers, not all of whom were appointed by the Supreme Director. For instance, all Bishops were ministers, and each university was required to select one doctor to serve as a minister. Two merchants and two *hacendados,* whose capital was not less than thirty thousand pesos, were to be appointed minister by the Chamber of Deputies. The Supreme Director was required to select the remaining ministers from specific places, such as the army. Assessed merely at the surface, the constitution surely gives the impression that a governing oligarchy was attempting to insure its own longevity. The term oligarchy is quite meaningless during the O'Higgins tenure, serving mostly to obscure the varied nature of the active citizenry: It was not monolithic, and the government created by the new organic law was intended to be fairly representative of it.

One should remember that it was not a question of liberal versus democratic ideology: The only negotiable point was how best to guarantee constitutional freedoms. The documents do not suggest that any Chileans were clamoring for such things as universal manhood suffrage. So sure were the liberals of their position, so uncontested was it, that in the election of Deputies they allowed all *vecinos*—neighbors—to vote in the municipal elections. The *cabildos* would select special electors at the ratio of one for every one thousand inhabitants, who in turn would elect the Deputies at the ratio of one for every fifteen thousand inhabitants. Surely the framers of the constitution did not propose that non-citizen residents of the municipalities should vote for Deputies. Even had they desired to establish such a radical precedent, the various *cabildos* would have frustrated the attempt at the local level. But there was no need to be specific: No one seems to have entertained the thought of enfranchising domestic servants, public debtors, and vagrants. This was the measure of the serene complacency in which the active citizenry lived.

Rather than a President, the constitution provided for a Supreme Director, whose faculties and limitations were similar to his counterpart in the United States. It was an elective position with a special note making it perfectly certain that it was not hereditary. The term of office was six years, but the Supreme Director could be re-elected for one four-year term. Nothing was said concerning the possibility of being re-elected after having been out of office for a term or more. In the future the legislature would elect the Supreme Director with a two-thirds majority, but for the present it was stipulated that O'Higgins would serve as Supreme Director with a full term beginning with the swearing of allegiance to the document.

The constitution officially divided Chile into the now standard three provinces, each to be administered by a governor-intendant. But the framers of the document desired to centralize administrative control more than in the past. Thus, the entire country was divided into departments, each to be governed by an official named by the Supreme Director "with the title directorial delegate." More than any aspect of the constitution this article led to the overthrow of the O'Higgins regime. The provinces of Concepción and Coquimbo were scandalized by this insidious attempt to undermine prerogatives, which since 1810 had begun to seem traditional. The spirit of regionalism inherent in the Spanish colonial system had been energized during the decade after 1810 when provincial juntas controlled their regions much as they chose.[3]

These highlights of the Constitution of 1822 should demonstrate just how patently liberal were the delegates at the Convention. Their central concern was constitutional government, the creation of an organic law that would guarantee individual freedoms. They were humanitarians in the sense that a pervasive sentiment of *noblesse oblige* compelled them to take an interest in the welfare of all members of society, but they were not democrats and were not inspired by supernal concepts of social reform. October was indeed a productive month for the O'Higgins administration. On its last day María Graham perhaps understated this in her journal: "This month has been a most important one for Chile. The government has promulgated its new constitution and its new commercial regulations, neither of which appear to me to answer their purpose." Actually, neither was given much chance.

Once the constitution was promulgated, O'Higgins' main problem was the irascible fleet at Valparaíso. So busy had he been during the last days of October that the Supreme Director had not even the time to care for his own health. To San Martín, at the moment luxuriating at the baths of Cauquenes, he wrote on the last day of October that he had to attend the sessions of the Convention quite ill. But this was of little concern compared to the threatened naval insurrection. He laid the blame at the corruption of naval officers and the lack of payments to both officers and sailors. Most distressing was that Lord Cochrane refused to intervene in the deteriorating situation on the grounds that his influence was not sufficient to eliminate the discontent produced by the shortage of money and basic necessities. O'Higgins reported that he would leave for the port on the morrow with some money for the fleet. Several days earlier he had sent two hundred and fifty soldiers to bolster the port's garrison, and he planned to take another hundred with him. "Already I have lost patience and nearly judgment too," he admitted. He was going to remove the crews from all the ships of the fleet and leave them in the care of trusted personnel. And, he resolved, resistance would be met with force.

On November 2 María Graham noted that news in Valparaíso indicated that the government was in earnest in its intentions to pay the squadron. On the third she recorded: "This evening, at about nine o'clock, the Supreme Director came quietly to the port." It was not clear to this perceptive observer exactly why in fact he came to the port. Ostensibly the trip was made to insure that the fleet was paid, but it was also known that San Martín was on his way from Cauquenes to Santiago, and it was rumored that the Director intended to avoid a personal meeting just at the moment. But it had also been suggested that O'Higgins came to the port to place Cochrane under arrest as a means of weakening the power of the fleet. A few days later she noted that the government's forces in Valparaíso were so few that they "would scarcely suffice to guard the Director, or to secure a state prisoner. . . ." Now she was quite sure that the true purpose of the visit was to seize her friend Cochrane.

Upon arriving at the port O'Higgins' attention was diverted from the task at hand—whatever it may have been. On November 4 a ship from Talcahuano reported the mournful news that not only had the south's agricultural crop failed, but hundreds of people already had died. O'Higgins immediately ordered a public subscription to be taken. Perhaps since the merchants of the port had given money for the same cause just shortly before, the subscription did not amount to much. However, it did focus attention away from the Supreme Director for a moment. On the twelfth Graham had more to say about the naval situation: "The squadron is in a way to be paid, though, perhaps, too late; but when the money came down, they forgot to send stamped paper to make out the tickets . . . so the officers and sailors must wait till proper paper can be stamped, and sent from Santiago for the purpose." A few days earlier she had confided to her journal: "I can hear that sort of covert voice of discontent that precedes civil strife." It was an accurate premonition.

On the nineteenth Valparaíso was struck by one of those natural catastrophes that all throughout Latin America during the early nineteenth century managed to confirm people in their superstitions and cause revolutionary movements and governments to falter. The port was visited by a major earthquake that destroyed a considerable part of the town. The governor of Valparaíso reported that much of the coast had been raised at least three feet over its previous level. Both Cochrane and O'Higgins did yeoman service in maintaining order and in giving direction to the rescue efforts. Even before the last tremors were felt, several port clergymen led a movement that blamed the calamity on the Supreme Director's religious toleration and the presence of foreign heretics in the country. However, others, such as Camilo Henríquez, denounced such irresponsible ignorance on the part of their fellow religious.

A week after the earthquake hit, O'Higgins retired to the capital, which had suffered little by comparison, in a state of utter exhaustion. He decided to proceed almost at once to his country residence for a period of recuperation. San Martín was there recovering from a fever, and O'Higgins may have felt it was time for the two comrades to commiserate with each other over their respective plights. One was without a job or a country to serve; the other had both but was fast losing them. Before departing he ordered government officials to stop all future processions intended to placate God, since these served merely to terrorize the population. This did much to preserve public order and inflate O'Higgins' non-religious image.

The revolution which toppled O'Higgins from power commenced in Concepción in November 1822. The south in general had many valid complaints against the government in Santiago. It had suffered the physical burden of the independence movement, and was receiving far less financial support from Santiago than it required. To make matters worse, descriptions of the many banquets tendered by the Supreme Director were not well received in poverty-stricken Concepción. It mattered not that these were perhaps unavoidable government obligations and that O'Higgins paid for them himself. Rodríguez Aldea's commercial restrictions and personal irregularities were carried out at the direct expense of the south, and they fired a developing antipathy.

The rumor that circulated in Concepción suggesting that Freire might be replaced by Luis de la Cruz did little to adhere Freire or the army to the government. All this alone probably would have been enough to incite a revolution, but when kindled by the October commercial regulation and constitution, both highly inimical to various influential groups in Concepción, the revolution was perhaps inevitable.

In late November Freire wrote to Cochrane deploring the desultory state of the nation, mentioning these very factors. He implored Cochrane to act, but did not ask him to join a particular movement. Taking advantage of the intramural warfare that continued to rage between Cochrane and San Martín, Freire managed to say some grievous things about the Argentine. But Cochrane was not to be baited so easily. He determined to remain aloof from the impending revolt, and he neither answered the letter nor let its contents be known. A few days later he did write to his friend O'Higgins, urging him to take into account the intense unrest abroad in the land and the jeopardy into which Rodríguez Aldea had placed the entire government. But he did not mention the letter from Freire. Before the end of the month Freire ordered all *cabildos* in Concepción to send delegates to a provincial assembly that he intended to convene in the city of Concepción on November 30. He stipulated that all Chileans, regardless of class or profession, should be allowed to vote. Since protest against Santiago was so universal, this democratic gesture was probably less altruistic than it has seemed to some, and more of an adroit political maneuver. And as it turned out, very few people eligible to vote actually did so. The Assembly met finally on December 9, at which time Intendant Freire renounced his position on the grounds that it pertained to a government that had made itself illegal. The renunciation was accepted, but on the following day the delegates voted him the same position in the name of the sovereign population which they represented. He accepted.[4]

Freire had judged that once the Assembly convened others would be called by the northern provinces. What is more, he seems to have counted on the support of Cochrane and the fleet. On both accounts he was to be disappointed. By the middle of December he and the Assembly turned to diplomacy. Letters were sent to San Martín by both. The Assembly requested that he induce O'Higgins to avert a civil war by convening a national assembly to deal with the problems facing the country. Freire was less temperate, calling for O'Higgins' resignation. On December

17 the Concepción forces backed up the provincial government's position by taking the strategic city of Talca. But the Supreme Director already had requested that the Court of Representatives grant him extraordinary powers, which it soon did.

While the fabric of nationhood that had been stitched together so laboriously during the past several years was tearing apart from within, the Chilean government was confronted by problems of considerable importance, which it faced with appreciable calm considering the circumstances. The most significant was the Irisarri loan. For some time now it had been known that Irisarri was attempting to negotiate a loan in London that would finance the *Expedición Libertadora* and the establishment of a government in Peru. But since he had not managed to do so, the matter never received prolonged discussion. And indeed there was much to discuss: Irisarri was never authorized to secure a loan. While the government could have used the money to finance its own security at the moment, its main concern was its international image. Irisarri signed a contract for a loan of one million pounds sterling, equivalent to five million pesos.

The money was to be raised by a bond issue, and these were placed on the London Exchange at between 70 and 72 per cent of face value. The loan was arranged and administered by Hullet Brothers, who charged 1½ per cent. Irisarri took 2 per cent for his services. That left the Chilean government with about 67½ per cent of the value upon which they were required to pay an interest of 6 per cent and an amortization of 1 per cent. On the same day in mid-December that O'Higgins asked the Court of Representatives to grant him extraordinary powers, the legislature appointed a commission to decide whether it would be lawful to rescind the contract. Six days later, on the nineteenth, the Court of Representatives approved the loan, but the O'Higgins government never received money from it. Probably its most enduring result was the manner in which businessmen were allured into politics in order to protect their new interests created by the loan. Called the *estanqueros,* they formed the nucleus of the political grouping known as the *pelucones,* who ended the years of instability which followed the fall of O'Higgins and established an environment of peace and order after their revolution of 1829.

On December 14 United States Agent Prevost wrote to Secretary Adams that the province of Concepción indeed was in a revolutionary mood, but he believed that if the central government financed the reconstruction of the south a civil war could be stifled. Perhaps it was wise to station a second diplomat outside the capital, where a different perspective might be obtained: Consul Hogan observed just two days later that Freire, whom he called "the most popular man in Chile," already had mobilized his troops. In Valparaíso, where sentiment against the commercial regulations was great, a civil war seemed more likely than it may have in Santiago. On December 22 O'Higgins offered to name a three-man deputation fully empowered to negotiate a settlement to meet with a delegation representing Concepción. On January 3 the Concepción Assembly agreed. The two sides were supposed to meet on January 22.

But while the Concepción Assembly contemplated the peace offer, the province of Coquimbo formed its own assembly and declared its allegiance to Concepción. Shortly thereafter, the *cabildo* of La Serena, also in the north, convoked an assembly and declared its support of the Concepción movement. Other towns followed suit. The two men who might have arranged a peace chose to remain neutral. At the end of December 1822, San Martín left Chile for good, and in the middle of January Lord Cochrane did likewise.

Further peace efforts were made during January 1823. Minister Rodríguez Aldea presented his resignation on January 7, and the following day the Supreme Director reluctantly accepted it. O'Higgins wrote personally to his friend Freire on the fourteenth. It was an emotional letter, moving in its sincerity, and warmly ironic in its effect. In fact, were it not for O'Higgins' acknowledged honesty and profound love of country, one could consider it a satire on Chilean politics. As one would expect, there was the initial statement of friendship: "How have you forgotten that I have been your greatest friend . . . ?" The letter centered on O'Higgins' electoral procedures and Freire's reaction to them. "It is true," he allowed, "that I wanted good men, steady and separate from any party." It was, he observed, the obligation of every government to guarantee order and tranquility. To O'Higgins, it was obviously proper to secure this through the manipulation of elections. And as a classical liberal he found much practical authority for his position. After all, even Popes were not elected by an open, popular election. And then the irony. Speaking of the recent election of the Concepción Assembly, he chided: "Do you believe that I am ignorant as to how the assembly of that province has been elected? I know it all and I keep quiet so as not to offend our friendship." It is more than likely that O'Higgins' appraisal of Concepción's electoral techniques was accurate, that Freire employed the very same tactics he deplored in O'Higgins.

On January 18, 1823, the government's delegates departed for the south. The Court of Representatives met for the last time on the twenty-second. On the twenty-fifth Miguel Zañartu returned from Buenos Aires after having served there for some time as the Chilean diplomatic deputy. O'Higgins felt that he would add prestige to the government delegation and be well received by his friend Freire, so on the same day that he arrived in Santiago O'Higgins authorized him to travel immediately to the peace conference. Three days later, on January 28, O'Higgins resigned and turned over the powers of government to a three-man Junta.

The actual events surrounding the resignation constitute one of the most frequently told stories in Chilean history. Between ten and eleven in the morning of the twenty-eighth about sixty men met in Santiago to decide what to do about the Supreme Director. But they refused to proceed without some sort of assurance that reprisals would not be taken against them. Army Colonel Pereira personally guaranteed the neutrality of the meeting, but under the condition that O'Higgins' life be considered inviolable. Shortly the meeting expanded to about two hundred men. A commission of six councilmen and six residents was selected, and they proceeded to the directorial palace, where they asked O'Higgins to return with them to the meeting. His refusal was unexpected, and made some at least sorry that they had gotten involved in the whole affair. But the assembly responded by selecting an executive committee to act in its name. Its first act was to declare the person of the Supreme Director inviolable. Then its members marched over to the directorial palace and also requested the Director's presence at the general meeting. Again O'Higgins refused. In the following hours the meeting grew, and new delegations visited the Supreme Director. It was during this tense period that O'Higgins performed one of the most intrepid acts of his career. Learning that part of the local garrison had gone over to the side of the assembly, he left the secure confines of the palace and personally confronted the errant troops. The leader of one contingent he publicly cashiered in front of the troops, who were stunned into a realization of the enormity of their actions, and who immediately made protestations of loyalty. The second contingent followed their lead. Late in the afternoon General Luis de la Cruz convinced O'Higgins that the army was loyal, but also that the assembly was composed of respectable people and not a revolutionary mob. O'Higgins was persuaded, and proceeded to the assembly.

Much has been written about the dialogue between O'Higgins and the members of the assembly, but no primary accounts are available. Suffice to say that the Supreme Director carried himself with estimable calm and dignity. As a result of the meeting he agreed to resign, and a Junta was elected. Though not all accounts agree concerning exactly what O'Higgins said in his final speech, certain it is that his sincerity and passion stirred the population and might well have made it possible for him to resume control should he have chosen to do so. On the following day a provisional organic law of twenty-three articles was published.

O'Higgins quickly made plans to leave the country. He arrived at Valparaíso on February 6, but was not permitted to depart for quite some time.

Thus, six years of government drew to a close in a matter of hours, caused by civilians and effected without the quota of bloodshed usually attendant upon such alterations. On the balance his was a successful administration. Most significant of all, perhaps, is that he created a working governmental organization. The central needs of the new nation, peace and order, were provided. Schools had been opened throughout the country, the Maipo Canal completed, and a theater in Santiago opened. And even steam navigation had been attempted. Under adverse circumstances the most powerful national navy of any Pacific American state was created and launched. Moreover, under equally hostile conditions, a major military expedition was mounted, transported and for a while supported financially. Perhaps O'Higgins' most impressive successes were on the diplomatic front. There he displayed a greater acuity than when dealing with domestic matters. Though the United States did not recognize Chile specifically, as was hoped would be the case, its general recognition of Latin American states in 1822 included Chile. Certainly, it was disappointing that Great Britain had not yet followed this example, but the Irisarri loan, with all its drawbacks, indicated that the British financial community was relatively confident of the permanency of Chilean independence. But in domestic politics O'Higgins was less successful.

After 1820 the country needed a leader with a more instinctive touch and actually did not get him until after 1829. Even before the *Expedición Libertadora* sailed in August 1820, O'Higgins had antagonized the Church and aristocracy. Later he alienated the business community. Writing after O'Higgins' death, General José María de la Cruz, the son of Luis de la Cruz and one of O'Higgins' most loyal supporters, observed perceptively that the Supreme Director governed without any party at all. His only support was the risk of war and the army: Once this risk disappeared . . . "the fall of O'Higgins was inevitable. . . ." [5] However true this may have been, the circumstances were somewhat more complicated than Cruz may have judged. For one thing, the Director's lack of support was the immediate result of his repugnant association with the Argentine continental plan. It would appear that elements of the active citizenry would have drifted away from him even had he not given them direct cause. It is not possible to estimate how much support he would have had if he were able to project a more forceful image as a *national* leader, but certainly it would have been more than the few loyal advocates with whom he ended his career. Altogether, however, one must agree with Cruz. Whatever the reasons for his want of support, the fact remains that after 1820 his administrative shortcomings portended ill for a long tenure.

Notwithstanding his liberalism O'Higgins was a dictator. Though civil liberties were guaranteed, they were not always respected. But when compared to the later totalitarian dictatorships his was not very malevolent. O'Higgins believed his actions were in strict accordance with the precepts of good government as practiced throughout the western world. He did not delude himself into thinking his title "Supreme" was merely decorative. He was a partisan of strong central government, and for his inspiration he turned to the most respectable places. Though some of his statements of ideology were at best vague, one can conclude that he was a classical liberal.

Again Cruz: "His political principles were republican and democratic, but not of that democracy that endeavors to submit the exercise of public administration to the general public." Thus, he believed that the exercise of public administration pertained to those sensible and capable of independent thought.[6] Remembering that Cruz wrote these comments a few years after the 1848 February Revolution in France took place and educated a whole generation of young Chileans in the concepts of democracy, and thus gave democracy its first significant vogue in Chile, they are indeed accurate. The introduction of the term democracy into his observations is unfortunate and was the result of his desire to lend respectability to O'Higgins' political ideology at a time when democracy had captured the imagination of the Chilean intellectual community and anything else was suspect. What Cruz might have said is that O'Higgins was a republican and a liberal, but not a democrat as the term was understood in the 1820's. This would not have been an entirely unworthy epithet.

CHAPTER VIII

Exile

THOUGH THE DELEGATES REPRESENTING SANTIAGO AND CONCEPCIÓN who met at Quechereguas on January 29 for the first time did not know it, part of their work already had been accomplished for them by O'Higgins. Both sides were agreed that the Supreme Director would have to resign to preserve the peace. The only negotiable point was the type of government that should succeed him. Strangely, the delegates from Concepción desired that a junta representing the three provinces be selected to govern provisionally, while those from Santiago argued that a single provisional Director be appointed and that he be Freire. The Santiago delegates preferred to turn over power to the southern general and intendant rather than chance embarrassing the system of competent central government. Yet the delegates from Concepción temporized. On the following day, Zañartu arrived at the conference and attempted to convince the southerners that the cause of peace would be served best through the selection of Freire as provisional Director. The Concepción delegates answered that they would have to confer with their Assembly on such a portentous issue, and they departed for the south. Freire was eventually elected provisional Director and Supreme Chief by a Congress of Plenipotentiaries on March 31. On April 3 the provincial Assembly of Santiago approved.

O'Higgins and Freire both arrived at Valparaíso on February 6. O'Higgins was quartered in a government residence and treated respectfully. But before Freire docked, he sent ashore a communication ordering O'Higgins' arrest. Colonel Jorge Beauchef was charged with carrying out the order. Reluctantly, Beauchef separated O'Higgins' escort from their duties and then personally visited the former Director. After a fairly pleasant conversation the two rode over to General Freire's camp, and O'Higgins was received. The erstwhile comrades met two more times in the succeeding days. The result of all of which was that O'Higgins remained in a sort of moderate house arrest.

In early March he wrote to San Martín that the arrest had

been suspended. His only inconvenience now was the anxiety of waiting for permission to depart. "England will be the country of my residence, if, as is just, I am conceded permission." During the following month his good spirits degenerated into morose pessimism. To San Martín he wrote in April that he was not sure there were any tortures to which his spirit had not been subjected. It was not a time for restraint: "Death would have been kinder than days of such affliction." And as for the country itself: "Anarchy, ambition and confusion destroy our labors. . . ." In April he wrote: "Greatly have I celebrated the naming of our b:: and friend Freire to the Directorate, since only thusly would the limitless pretensions of the Provinces that precipitated the country to its ruin be able to be calmed." It is quite remarkable that so long after the *Logia lautarina* ceased to exert influence in Chile O'Higgins would invoke the cryptic alternative for the word "brother." But the statement is also a measure of his compelling sincerity and immutable belief in the propriety of a strong central government. The humiliation inflicted upon him by Freire would have caused a lesser man to seek retribution.

Throughout February and March the government did not see fit to present O'Higgins with his passports so that he could leave the country. In early April a movement was begun by his political enemies to subject him to a *residencia,* the legal procedure that would involve an examination of his public acts and perhaps an indictment and actual trial. According to the Constitution of 1818 the Supreme Director in most cases was not responsible for his official acts. On April 21 the Senate ruled that O'Higgins was in fact responsible for the acts of his government which were decreed by him alone, for the naming of his ministers, and for acting contrary to the advice of the Senate on constitutional questions. On the same day a *tribunal de residencia* was appointed. A considerable propaganda, some defending O'Higgins, some condemning him, now made its way into public view. But no matter how heated the debate grew, O'Higgins remained aloof from the discussion and kept his silence. Toward the end of June the tribunal decided that since O'Higgins' life was declared inviolable and since he still held property in Chile, it would be proper to allow him to leave the country. In early July the Senate agreed. Minister Mariano Egaña immediately wrote an official note to O'Higgins, which was designed to serve as his passport. It contained the most complimentary statements about the former Director.

O'Higgins planned to take up residence in Great Britain and even made arrangements to sail on a British merchant ship about to leave Valparaíso. However, it was winter now and the trip around the Cape would have been unnecessarily dangerous for his family. Though never married he did manage to acquire a family, and in much the same manner as did his father. His natural son Pedro Demetrio O'Higgins was his companion in exile and the last of the line started, although unconventionally, by Ambrosio Higgins. On July 13 the British corvette "Fly" docked at Valparaíso en route to Callao. The ship's Captain graciously offered to transport O'Higgins and his family to Callao, Peru. On the seventeenth O'Higgins departed on a trip that he thought would take him eventually to Europe. He not only never got to Europe, he never returned to Chile. His exile lasted nineteen years.

The party arrived at Callao on July 25. O'Higgins wrote at once to the Chilean representative in Peru, indicating that he intended to travel to Ireland, where he hoped to live for a while. He asked the diplomat to intervene on his behalf with the Peruvian government so that he would be permitted to remain in Peru for a short while. The President of patriot Peru, José Bernardo de Tagle, an old Lima schoolmate of his, answered the same day that the ship docked that he was a welcome guest in Peru, free to remain as long as he liked and free to travel and reside in whatever part of the country he desired.

In August O'Higgins wrote to San Martín from Lima of his new happiness: "Already I begin to enjoy all the tranquility that an individual independence can provide. . . ." There was also the bitter note that would be characteristic of his attitude all during the period of exile: "and, far from ungratefuls and cowards, I enjoy in sweet calm the satisfactory reflection of a sound conscience, without the vexation of any aspiration." Then in a sadly revealing passage he observed that Peru had fallen into a state of disorder and suggested that all the people lamented the absence "of their best father and liberator. . . ." He assured San Martín that his name continued to enjoy an excellent reputation and that presently thousands of people already were preparing for his return. The impression one gets from reading the letter is that O'Higgins hoped for similar circumstances in Chile. In 1822 San Martín's government in Peru had granted O'Higgins the haciendas of Curiba and Montalván, both quite some distance to the south of Lima, as a reward for his services in the liberation of the country. As it turned out, this was indeed a fortuitous gift. However, now O'Higgins told his benefactor that both haciendas had been ruined completely by the enemy. If he could rent them, he would proceed to Panama and then on to Great Britain.

O'Higgins spent the remaining months of 1823 attempting to make arrangements for the disposal of his haciendas and to provide for himself and his family. The year 1824 proved to be more satisfying and exciting than he might have hoped. Now Simón Bolívar was preparing the final thrust against the continent's remaining royalists. In 1824 he was at once Liberator and President of Colombia, and Supreme Dictator of Peru. O'Higgins let it be known that he wanted to fight alongside the great Liberator. Writing in 1855 in answer to several questions posed by Diego Barros Arana, General José María de la Cruz noted that when O'Higgins first arrived in Peru his relations with Bolívar were not noticeably cordial, but they developed into something friendly.[1] Bolívar desired every advantage possible and appreciated the positive influence O'Higgins' presence would have on morale. Initially he contemplated sending O'Higgins back to Chile to gather an expeditionary force that would join in the final confrontation. How much he overestimated O'Higgins' position at home!

The former Supreme Director's demeaning life in exile took on a new and welcome aspect in June 1824, when Bolívar actually offered him a command in his army. O'Higgins accepted eagerly and enthusiastically: "What a flattering thing it is for an Araucanian soldier to be invited into the ranks of his brave brothers from Colombia!" He made it clear that he would be quick to follow all orders given by the Liberator. It took O'Higgins well over a month to arrive at Bolívar's headquarters. The years of constant warfare had depleted the country's supply of horses and mules, and he had a difficult time obtaining the number required to transport him to the war. However, the timing was less than perfect for one who was anxious to enter battle once again. On August 6, before O'Higgins joined the patriot forces, the royalists were defeated in an important battle on the plains of Junín. On September 1 O'Higgins wrote to his mother that he was encamped with Bolívar only twenty leagues from the enemy. But he did not expect an immediate battle, since the defeat at Junín had been so demoralizing to the enemy. The difficult march over a distance of several hundred miles across imposing terrain had reinvigorated him. His spirits were indeed high. His health was excellent, and he could hardly wait for the final battle to begin so that at least one Araucanian would witness the conclusion of the liberation movement. One must wonder if this reference to an Araucanian heritage was entirely rhetorical.

By the end of September the Liberator's army was on the march. It was exciting for O'Higgins. To Camilo Henríquez, he expressed this virile enthusiasm: "You, I do not doubt, will hear with sincere satisfaction that my health has gained so much in the present campaign, that I feel as young as in the days of Chillán, El Roble, Los Angeles, El Quilo, Gomero, Maule, Talca, Quechereguas, Rancagua, Chacabuco and Maipú. . . ." His sword until death, would be naked against the enemy. Again, as in the Chilean campaigns, he was a man with a mission. It seemed evident to him that the republics of America represented the vanguard of liberty for the entire world. Speaking of the inhabitants of the Peruvian hinterland, he observed that they were practically savages, and in doing so said much about his own philosophy. "Commerce is the most executive instrument of civilization, and the merchants with their games of glass and their utensils of iron effect more rapidly the task than the missionaries with their breviaries . . . and discipline." This is perhaps a not unlikely position for a classical liberal to take. In fact, businessmen and liberals were soon to find a mutual attraction in Chile. When the years of instability initiated by the resignation of O'Higgins terminated in 1829, the new order was produced by liberals like Mariano Egaña and merchants like Diego Portales. Many, including Portales, were both.

In the same letter O'Higgins spoke about America's indigenous population. So fundamental was his abhorrence of the Spanish heritage that he defended the Incaic social system. It, after all, produced a civilization conspicuously stable and free from the disorder which plagued most of the new states of America. Viewed in perspective this seemed to him a worthy achievement: It was accomplished at a time when the European powers "did not think of anything other than war, robbery and destruction." But more importantly, the tenacious system established by the Incas incorporated vassal nations that became much less ignorant and barbarous than neighboring nations. Thus it would appear that the lesson is that peace, order, and civilization justify the application of force and exonerate one from any ancillary evils. It is difficult to escape the conclusion that O'Higgins was vindicating his own approach to government and, perhaps unintentionally, suggesting a future course for Chile.

The year 1824 did not end with quite the flourish O'Higgins

doubtless anticipated. Owing to the exigencies of war, neither O'Higgins nor Bolívar took part in the Battle of Ayacucho, which occurred in early December and brought to an end the military war for independence as conceived by both Bolívar and San Martín. The patriots won the battle and the war, but it was General Sucre who took the final laurels, not the Liberator.

From the beginning of 1825 until his death in October 1842, O'Higgins lived a rather pathetic existence. He spent his time between the hacienda Montalván and Lima. In significant respects his last years manifest a poignant similarity to his first years. As a youth circumstances required that he live away from his home in Chillán, part of which time included lengthy stays in Peru and Europe. Now in his maturity circumstances again conspired to restrict him from residence at home. But a more striking similarity between the two periods was the state of dismal penury in which he found himself. However, though sufficient evidence is not available, it is likely that his property in Peru began to support his needs quite some time before his death.

Of itself this would not exude pathos. Had his friends left him alone, he might have adjusted to a new and not entirely unpleasant way of life. However, from 1825 on plans were made to return him to Chile, plans which animated his imagination and rendered his adopted country inevitably a foreign environment. O'Higgins listened to the plans, believed them, and on various occasions made ready to depart for a triumphal entrance into Chile. He himself swore never to return to Chile, but his letters indicate that this was probably a matter of pride. During his last years he was involved in plans to improve conditions in Chile. He desired to bring civilization to the Indian population of Chile, "to confer upon the Araucanians and other indigenous tribes the sweetnesses and benedictions of Christianity, good government and social industry." In early 1842 he spoke of his impending trip to Chile. Previously, the Chilean government had blocked efforts to recall O'Higgins, but now he was sixty-three years old and in failing health. He thought he would spend only the summer in Chile, so poor was his health. But he did not go. In June he wrote a letter to a correspondent in England in which he discussed his plans to improve the port of Valparaíso. He died at the port of Callao in October. His last months had been spent in Lima and then Callao. He had no reason to live so many months in Callao unless he truly planned to board a ship for Chile. His plans to return to Chile, his plans to improve his homeland, these ended by being merely dreams.

In the long run, perhaps these dreams made life in exile more tolerable than it might have been otherwise. But this is impossible to tell.

Notes and References

INTRODUCTION

1. Jay Kinsbruner, *Diego Portales: Interpretative Essays on the Man and Times* (The Hague, 1967), 7.

2. A similar view is presented in Jaime Eyzaguirre, *Ideario y ruta de la emancipación Chilena* (Santiago, 1957), 57.

3. This view is not original with the present writer. It was stated by W. G. D. Worthington in a letter to John Quincy Adams, Secretary of State, dated Santiago, July 4, 1818. In William R. Manning (ed.), *Diplomatic Correspondence of the United States. Concerning the Independence of the Latin-American Nations* (3 vols.; New York, 1925), II, 930–39. Hereinafter cited as *Correspondence.* Only volume II was used for this book.

4. Kinsbruner, *op. cit.,* 43–4.

CHAPTER I

1. This book relies on primary sources more than the general purposes of the series warrant. Thus it was thought appropriate to take four professional liberties. Bernardo O'Higgins' letters will not be footnoted, since they can be found rather conveniently in Ernesto de la Cruz (ed.), *Epistolario De D. Bernardo O'Higgins* (2 vols.; Santiago, 1916). Some letters located after 1916 are to be found in the *Archivo de don Bernardo O'Higgins* (Santiago, 1947–present), hereinafter cited as *Archivo.* Twenty-three volumes have been published thus far. All of O'Higgins' letters used in this book, except where noted, are my translations of letters written in Spanish or of Spanish translations of letters written originally in English. Also, the letters of United States diplomats, available in Manning's *Correspondence,* will not be footnoted. In addition, the sessions of the various legislatures, available in Valentín Letelier (ed.), *Sesiones de los cuerpos lejislativos de la república de Chile, 1811 a 1845* (37 vols.; Santiago, 1887–1908), hereinafter cited as *Sesiones,* will not be footnoted generally. Nor will the newspapers, conveniently collected in the Biblioteca Nacional's *Colección De Antiguos Periódicos Chilenos,* be footnoted, except under unusual circumstances.

A reliable account of O'Higgins' early life is "Antecedentes Biográficos de don Bernardo O'Higgins," in Diego Barros Arana, *Historia General De Chile* (2nd ed., 12 vols.; Santiago, 1930–41), XII, 535–62.

2. The original of this letter is not extant. One Spanish version is to be found in Benjamín Vicuña Mackenna, *El ostracismo del general d. Bernardo O'Higgins* (n.p., 1860), 50–53. For another version see *Archivo,* PRIMER APENDICE, 2–4.

3. Vicuña Mackenna, *op. cit.,* 54.

4. Barros Arana, *Historia General, op. cit.,* XII, 546.

CHAPTER II

1. Joseph De Gorbea Y Vadillo & Agustín Doría to Bernardo O'Higgins, Lima, October 22, 1802, in *Archivo,* I, 32.

2. Pedro Nolasco Del Río to Bernardo O'Higgins, Angeles, April 20, 1803, in *Archivo,* I, 34–35.

3. According to Diego Barros Arana, "Antecedentes Biográficos de don Bernardo O'Higgins," in Diego Barros Arana, *Historia General De Chile* (2nd ed., 12 vols.; Santiago, 1930–41), XII, 559, Bernardo feared imprisonment and a trip to Lima as a criminal of state.

4. *Archivo,* I, 36–38; 43–44. Also *Archivo,* PRIMER APENDICE, 8–9.

5. *Archivo,* I, 48–49; 50–52.

6. *Archivo,* I, 59–60.

7. *Archivo,* PRIMER APENDICE, 18–19.

8. Francisco A. Encina, *Historia De Chile* (20 vols.; Santiago, 1948–56), VI, 215.

9. See Hernán Ramírez Necochea, *Antecedentes económicos de la Independencia de Chile* (Santiago, 1959), 104.

10. Encina, *op. cit.,* VI, 185–87.

11. Encina, *op. cit.,* VI, 187–88.

12. "Convocación Al Congreso Nacional De 1811 Por La Junta De Gobierno, En 15 De Diciembre De 1810," in *Sesiones,* I, 9–11.

13. Juan Mackenna to Bernardo O'Higgins, Santiago, February 20, 1811, in *Archivo,* I, 70–104. The original of this letter is in English. My translation was made from a Spanish copy.

14. *Archivo,* I, 105–8.

15. "Poderes De Don Bernardo O'Higgins Y De Don José María Benavente, Diputados Por La Villa De Los Angeles," in *Archivo,* I, 109–12.

16. *Sesiones,* I, 12; 18.

17. *Archivo,* Primer Apendice, 20, footnote (1).

18. *Archivo,* I, 144–46.

19. See Barros Arana, *Historia General, op. cit.,* VIII, 392.

20. In *Archivo,* I, 113–15. The protest was signed on June 24 and presented on July 4.

21. Barros Arana, *Historia General, op. cit.,* VIII, 403.

22. *Sesiones,* I, 51.

23. "Exposición Que Con Fecha 12 De Agosto De 1811 . . . Explicando Los Motivos De Su Separación Voluntaria Del Congreso," in *Archivo,* I, 115–16.

24. "Exposición Que Hace El Diputado Don Bernardo O'Higgins . . . Explicando Los Motivos De Su Separación Voluntaria Del Congreso," in *Archivo,* I, 117–19.

25. "Circular Del Congreso A Las Provincias. Santiago 13 Agosto 1811," in *Archivo,* I, 119–27. The Congress held an interesting view of the electoral system in the United States. The President of the United States, the circular noted, "is elected . . . by all the provinces simultaneously . . ." (p. 121).

26. "Acta . . . De La Villa De Los Angeles, Reunido En Cabildo Abierto En 13 De Agosto De 1818," in *Archivo,* I, 130–33.

27. Act of the *cabildo abierto* of Los Angeles meeting on September 17, 1811, in *Archivo,* I, 134–40.

28. "Oficio De Don Bernardo O'Higgins . . ." (n.d.), in *Archivo,* I, 140–42.

29. "Puntos Que Hay Que Pedir A La Junta (por el Diputado don Bernardo O'Higgins)" (n.d.), in *Archivo,* I, 148–49.

30. "Proyecto Del Diputado O'Higgins" (n.d.), in *Archivo,* I, 146–48.

31. For a fascinating discussion of Carrera see Julio Alemparte, *Carrera Y Freire* (Santiago, 1963), 8–29 and *passim.*

32. "Oficio De Don Bernardo O'Higgins Al Presidente De La Junta Provincial De Concepción, En 21 De Noviembre De 1811 (Santiago)," in *Archivo,* I, 154–57.

33. See *Sesiones,* I, 185–90.

34. See *Sesiones,* I, 195–96.

35. *Archivo,* I, 157.

36. José Miguel Carrera to Señores de la Junta Provincial de Concepción, Santiago, December 4, 1811, in *Archivo,* PRIMER APENDICE, 66–69.

37. "Convención Entre Santiago Y Concepción," in *Archivo,* I, 181–86.

38. This is according to Barros Arana, *Historia General, op. cit,* IX, 80–81. Many of the documents relative to these negotiations are not extant, as Barros Arana observes. The present writer has not seen documents indicating Rozas' position.

39. In *Archivo,* I, 186; 187.

40. Cabildo Eclesiástico to Junta Gubernativa del Reino, Santiago, February 3, 1812, in *Archivo,* PRIMER APENDICE, 64–67.

41. Concepción Junta to Bernardo O'Higgins, Concepción, February 23, 1812, in *Archivo,* I, 188.

42. Barros Arana, *Historia General, op. cit.,* IX, 93–94.

43. Pedro José Benavente to Bernardo O'Higgins, Concepción, March 14, 1812, in *Archivo,* I, 189.

44. For this discussion I am following Diego Barros Arana, *Historia General, op. cit.,* IX, 94–115. He made use of documents that do not seem to be available today.

45. *Sesiones,* I, 259–61.

CHAPTER III

1. José Miguel Carrera to Bernardo O'Higgins, Talca, April 5, 1813, in *Archivo,* I, 217.

2. José Miguel Carrera to Bernardo O'Higgins, Talca, April 11, 1813, in *Archivo,* I, 227–28.

3. "Decreto De La Junta De Gobierno, De 8 De October De 1813," in *Sesiones,* I, 324–25.

4. Juan Mackenna to Bernardo O'Higgins, Concepción, November 16, 1813, in *Archivo,* I, 288–89.

5. "Oficio Del Cabildo De Concepción A La Excma. Junta De Gobierno," in *Archivo,* I, 301–4.

6. "Bando De La Junta De Gobierno," in *Archivo,* I, 304–8.

7. Junta De Gobierno to Bernardo O'Higgins, Talca, November 28, 1813, in *Archivo,* I, 312–13.

8. Again one must rely on Barros Arana, *Historia General De Chile* (2nd ed., 12 vols.; Santiago, 1930–41), X, 53.

9. "Acta de las Corporaciones," Santiago, December 4, 1813, in *Archivo,* I, 316–18.

10. Juan Mackenna to Bernardo O'Higgins, Talca, November 28, 1813, in *Archivo,* I, 310–12.

11. This is according to Barros Arana, *Historia General, op. cit.*, X, 65.

12. Junta De Gobierno to Gobernante Intendente de Santiago, Talca, December 9, 1813, in *Archivo*, I, 318.

13. Junta de Gobierno to Bernardo O'Higgins, Talca, February 1, 1814, in *Archivo*, II, 27–28.

14. Juan Mackenna to Bernardo O'Higgins, Quirihue, February 8, 1814, in *Archivo*, II, 51–52.

15. Junta de Gobierno to Bernardo O'Higgins, Talca, February 12, 1814, in *Archivo*, II, 71.

16. Junta De Gobierno to Bernardo O'Higgins, Talca, February 19, 1814, in *Archivo*, II, 73.

17. Junta De Gobierno to Bernardo O'Higgins, Talca, February 22, 1814, in *Archivo*, II, 67–68.

18. Letters in *Archivo*, II, 75–77.

19. "Reglamento Para El Gobierno Provisional," in *Sesiones*, I, 335–36.

20. Juan Mackenna to Bernardo O'Higgins, Membrillar, March 14, 1814, in *Archivo*, II, 111.

21. Bernardo O'Higgins to Junta De Gobierno, Campamento de Ranquil, March 21, 1814, in *Archivo* II, 113–15. Mackenna's letter is quoted by O'Higgins.

22. Juan Mackenna to Bernardo O'Higgins, Membrillar, March 22, 1814, in *Archivo*, II, 123.

23. Diego Barros Arana is one who feels that all the mitigating factors do not relieve O'Higgins from the responsibility of not having joined Mackenna sooner. See *Historia General, op. cit.*, X, 168.

24. The Treaty of Lircay is in *Archivo*, II, 138–41.

25. "Convenio Celebrado Entre Los Generales De Los Ejércitos Titulados Nacional Y Del Gobierno De Chile," in *Archivo*, II, 156–59.

26. Francisco Encina maintains that both sides signed the treaty in bad faith. See *Historia De Chile* (20 vols.; Santiago, 1948–56), X, 241; 254.

27. Quoted in Diego Barros Arana, *Historia General, op. cit.*, X, 264.

28. Statement in *Archivo*, II, 303–9.

29. Proceedings in *Archivo*, II, 310–17.

30. Statement in *Archivo*, II, 317–18.

31. For much of this discussion I am relying again on Diego Barras Arana, who had access to documents that are no longer available. See *Historia General, op. cit.*, X, 291–93.

32. This and the following paragraphs are based also on information presented by Barros Arana, *Historia General, op. cit.*, X, 335–42.

33. "Manifesto De Los Generales Del Ejército A Sus Conciudadanos Y Compañeros De Armas," Santiago, September 4, 1814, in *Archivo*, II, 344–46.

34. Quoted in Diego Barros Arana, *Historia General, op. cit.*, X, 356.

35. Barros Arana, *Historia General, op. cit.*, 356, footnote 24.

36. There is some discussion as to who actually wrote the note. See *Archivo*, II, 42, and Barros Arana, *Historia General, op. cit.*, X, 373, footnote 38.

37. See *Archivo*, II, 420.

38. For O'Higgins' account see *Archivo*, II, 420–27. It has even been suggested that Carrera sent O'Higgins a verbal message that he should charge out of the plaza while Carrera carried out a diversionary attack. After holding for some time, according to this argument, Carrera finally retreated. See Julio Alemparte, *Carrera Y Freire* (Santiago, 1963), 120–22.

CHAPTER IV

1. Ignacio Alvarez to Bernardo O'Higgins, Buenos Aires, January 20, 1816, in *Archivo,* VII, 15–16.
2. The several notes are in *Archivo,* VII, 20–22.
3. The pertinent documents can be found in *Archivo,* VII, 23–27.
4. "Diario," in *Archivo,* VII, 35–39.
5. "Plan De Campaña Para Atacar, Destruir Y Exterminar A Los Tiranos Usurpadores De Chile," in *Archivo,* VII, 64–79.
6. See *Archivo,* PRIMER APENDICE, 264–72.
7. San Martín to Supremo Director del Estado, Chacabuco, February 12, 1817, in *Archivo,* VII, 133.
8. San Martín to Señor Gobernador Intendente de la Provincia de Cuyo, Santiago, February 14, 1817, in *Archivo,* VII, 134.
9. The pertinent documents are in *Archivo,* VII, 159–61.
10. See his letter to Juan Florencia Terrada, written at the Cordillera de los Patos on January 30, 1817, in *Archivo,* VIII, 219–220.

CHAPTER V

1. *Cabildo* of Santiago to Señor Ministro de Estado, Santiago, June 18, 1817, in *Archivo,* XXII, 24–26.
2. See Diego Barros Arana, *Historia General De Chile* (2nd ed., 12 vols.; Santiago, 1930–41), XII, 68–69.
3. Francisco Ruiz Tagle to Bernardo O'Higgins, Santiago, February 23, 1817, in *Archivo,* VII, 185–86.
4. *Gaceta De Santiago De Chile,* September 6, 1817.
5. Juan Pablo Fretes to Bernardo O'Higgins, Buenos Aires, March 9, 1817, in *Archivo,* VII, 198–201.
6. Barros Arana, *Historia General, op. cit.,* 152–56.
7. Barros Arana, *Historia General, op. cit.,* 160–61.
8. Circular in *Archivo,* XXI, 16–17.
9. San Martín to Bernardo O'Higgins, Santiago, June 1, 1817, in *Archivo,* XXI, 72.
10. Diego Paroissien to Bernardo O'Higgins, Concepción, May 21, 1817, in *Archivo,* XXI, 243.
11. Much of this diplomatic discussion is based on Ricardo Montaner Bello, *Historia diplomática de la Independencia de Chile* (Santiago, 1961), *passim.*
12. Captain Samuel Hill of Ship Ophelia, "Journal And Log Book, Ophelia & Packet, 1815–1822," MS in Manuscript Division, New York Public Library. I updated the grammar of this selection somewhat.
13. Samuel Haigh, *Sketches of Buenos Ayres and Chile* (London, 1829), 228.
14. Bolívar's celebrated "Jamaica Letter" in Harold A. Bierck, Jr. and Vicente Lecuna (eds.), *Selected Writings of Bolívar* (2 vols.; New York, 1951), 103–22.
15. Haigh, *op. cit.,* 246.
16. Miguel Zañartu to W. G. D. Worthington, Santiago, April 20, 1818, in *Correspondence,* II, 921–23.
17. For the Constitution of 1818 see *Sesiones,* II, 9–18.
18. For a brilliant discussion of O'Higgins as a monarchist see Julio Alemparte, *Carrera Y Freire* (Santiago, 1963), 211–20.

19. *Archivo,* III, xi–xv.

20. Quoted in Francisco A. Encina, *Historia De Chile* (20 vols.; Santiago, 1948–56), VIII, 7.

21. Thomas Cochrane, *Narrative of Services in the Liberation of Chili . . .* (2 vols.; London, 1859), I, 2–4.

22. Tomás Guido to San Martín, Santiago, March 18, 1819, quoted in Ernesto de la Cruz (ed.), *Epistolario De D. Bernardo O'Higgins . . .* (2 vols.; Santiago, 1916), I, 213–18, footnote 1.

23. Antonio José de Irisarri to Señor Secretario de Estado en el Departamento de Relaciones Exteriores, Liverpool, July 21, 1819, in *Archivo,* III, 37–41.

24. For this discussion I am relying largely upon Montaner Bello, *op. cit.,* 87–95.

25. *Gaceta Ministerial De Chile,* October 23, 1819.

26. Gilbert F. Mathison, *Narrative of a Visit to Brazil, Chile, Peru . . .* (London, 1825), 206.

CHAPTER VI

1. Captain Samuel Hill of Ship Ophelia, "Journal And Log Book, Ophelia & Packet, 1815–1822," MS in Manuscript Division, New York Public Library.

2. San Martín to Bernardo O'Higgins, Lima, September 23, 1821, in *Archivo,* PRIMER APENDICE, 310–11.

3. This and the following two paragraphs are dependent on information presented in Diego Barros Arana, *Historia General De Chile* (16 vols.; Santiago, 1884–1902), XIII, 569–77; 709–12.

4. José Antonio De Irisarri to Señor Ministro Secretario de Estado y de Relaciones Exteriores, London, January 28, 1822, in *Archivo,* III, 322–28.

5. José Antonio de Irisarri to Señor Ministro Secretario de Estado y de Relaciones Exteriores, London, May 10, 1822, in *Archivo,* III, 335–47.

6. María Graham, *Journal of a Residence in Chile . . .* (London, 1824), 207–8.

CHAPTER VII

1. María Graham, *Journal of a Residence in Chile . . .* (London, 1824), 273–345.

2. For the Constitution of 1822 see *Sesiones,* V, 332–43.

3. For a comparison of the Constitution of 1822 with the liberal Spanish Constitution of 1812 see Eugenio Orrego Vicuña, *El espíritu constitucional de la administración O'Higgins* (Santiago, 1924), 179–204.

4. For this discussion of the Concepción revolution I am relying on Diego Barros Arana, *Historia General De Chile* (16 vols.; Santiago, 1884–1902), XIII, 783–97.

5. José María de la Cruz, *Recuerdos de Don Bernardo O'Higgins* (Santiago, 1960), 73–77.

6. *Ibid.,* 73.

CHAPTER VIII

1. José María de la Cruz, *Recuerdos de Don Bernardo O'Higgins* (Santiago, 1960), 138–39.

Selected Bibliography

PRIMARY SOURCES

Archivo de don Bernardo O'Higgins. Santiago: Imprenta Universitaria, 1947–present. (23 volumes have been published to date.)

Colección De Historiadores I De Documentos Relativos A La Independencia De Chile. 40 vols. Santiago: Imprenta Cervantes, 1900–present.

Diplomatic Correspondence of the United States. Concerning the Independence of the Latin-American Nations. Ed. William R. Manning. 3 vols. New York: Oxford University Press, 1925.

Epistolario De D. Bernardo O'Higgins. Capitán General Y Director Supremo De Chile . . . ed. Ernesto de la Cruz. 2 vols. Santiago: Imprenta Universitaria, 1916–19.

Jurisprudencia De La Cancilleria Chileana Hasta 1865 . . . ed. Alberto Cruchaga Ossa. Santiago: Imprenta Chile, 1935.

Selected Writings of Bolívar. Eds. Harold A. Bierck, Jr. and Vicente Lecuna. 2 vols. New York: The Colonial Press Inc., 1951.

Sesiones De Los Cuerpos Lejislativos De La República De Chile, 1811 A 1845. Ed. Valentín Letelier. 37 vols. Santiago: Imprenta Cervantes, 1887–1908.

Newspapers

The following newspapers published in Santiago and since republished by the Biblioteca Nacional in volumes under the title *Colección De Antiguos Periódicos Chilenos* were used:

El Argos De Chile, 1818.

El Cosmopolita, 1822.

El Duende De Santiago, 1818.

Gaceta Ministerial De Chile, 1818–23. (Between February 26, 1817 and June 11, 1817, the paper was called *Viva La Patria! Gaceta Del Supremo Gobierno De Chile*. Between July 18, 1817 and March 21, 1818, it was called *Gaceta De Santiago De Chile*.)

Gaceta Del Supremo Gobierno De Chile, 1817.

El Mercurio De Chile, 1822–23.

El Observador Chileno, 1822.

El Telégrafo, 1819–20.

TRAVEL ACCOUNTS AND MEMOIRS

COCHRANE, THOMAS. *Narrative of Services in the Liberation of Chili, Peru, and Brazil* . . . 2 vols. London: James Ridgway, 1859.

COFFIN, ISSAC FOSTER. *Journal of a Residence in Chile by a Young American* . . . Boston: Wells And Lilly, 1823.

CRUZ, JOSÉ MARÍA DE LA. *Recuerdos de Don Bernardo O'Higgins.* Santiago: Editorial Andrés Bello, 1960.

GRAHAM, MARÍA. *Journal of a Residence in Chile, During the Year 1822.* London: Longman *et al.,* 1824.

HAIGH, SAMUEL. *Sketches of Buenos Ayres and Chile.* London: James Carpenter and Son, 1829.

HILL, CAPTAIN SAMUEL. "Journal And Log Book, Ophelia & Packet, 1815–1822." MS in Manuscript Division, New York Public Library.

MATHISON, GILBERT F. *Narrative of a Visit to Brazil, Chile, Peru, and the Sandwich Islands, During the Years 1821 and 1822.* London: Charles Knight, 1825.

MIERS, JOHN. *Travels In Chile And La Plata* . . . 2 vols. London: Baldwin, Cradock, And Joy, 1826.

MILLER, GENERAL WILLIAM. *Memoirs of General William Miller in the Service of the Republic of Peru.* Ed. John Miller, 2nd ed., 2 vols.; London: Longman, Rees *et al.,* 1829.

SUTCLIFFE, THOMAS. *Sixteen Years in Chile and Peru* . . . London: Fischer, Son, and Co., 1841.

STEVENSON, W. B. *Historical and Descriptive Narrative of Twenty Years Residence in South America.* 3 vols. London: Longman, Rees *et al.,* 1829.

SECONDARY SOURCES

There have been surprisingly few recent studies devoted entirely to O'Higgins. Those that have appeared do not entirely supersede earlier works. Here are some of the more important secondary sources that may interest the reader.

ALEMPARTE, JULIO. *Carrera Y Freire.* Santiago: Editorial Nascimento, 1963. An illuminating evaluation of both figures with many interesting comments about O'Higgins.

AMUNÁTEGUI, MIGUEL LUIS and VICUÑA MACKENNA, BENJAMÍN. *La Dictadura De O'Higgins.* Madrid: Editorial América, n.d. First published in 1853, this book attempts to demonstrate that O'Higgins desired to establish a dictatorship in Chile. The problem being that dictatorship was not compatible with the environment.

BARROS ARANA, DIEGO. *Historia General De Chile.* 16 vols. Santiago: various publishers, 1884–1902. (Between 1930 and 1941, the Editorial Nascimento published a second edition of the first twelve volumes of this majestic study.) An even, balanced account, this remains the standard work on Chilean history through the middle of the nineteenth century. A special section entitled "Antecedentes Biográficos de don Bernardo O'Higgins," appears in volume XII, pp. 535–62 as an appendix. It is an excellent summation of information presented in the body.

DÍAZ VALDERRAMA, FRANCISCO JAVIER. *O'Higgins.* Buenos Aires: Círculo Militar, 1946. Concentrates on the military aspects of O'Higgins' career.

EDWARDS VIVES, ALBERTO. *La fronda aristocrática.* 5th ed. Santiago: Editorial

Del Pacifico, S. A., 1959. First published in 1928, this is an important study by one of Chile's leading modern conservatives.

ENCINA, FRANCISCO A. *Historia De Chile. Desde la prehistoria hasta 1891.* 20 vols. Santiago: Editorial Nascimento, 1948–56. Encina has something to say concerning just about everything. It is not always easy to agree, but it is always easy to enjoy.

EYZAGUIRRE, JAIME. *O'Higgins.* 3rd ed. Santiago: Editorial Zig-Zag, S. A., 1950. First published in 1945, this prize-winning book is the best recent biography of O'Higgins. Eyzaguirre is strongly pro-Church, and he generally finds it difficult to fault his subject.

FIGUEROA, PEDRO PABLO. *Diccionario Biográfico De Estranjeros En Chile.* Santiago: Imprenta Moderna, 1900. A very useful tool.

FIGUEROA, VIRGILIO. *Diccionario Histórico Y Biográfico De Chile.* 5 vols. Santiago: various publishers, 1925–31.

GALDAMES, LUIS. *A History Of Chile.* Trans. and ed. by Isaac Joslin Cox. Chapel Hill: The University of North Carolina Press, 1941. One of Chile's foremost historians presents a well-balanced, general account of his country's history.

GAY, CLAUDIO. *Historia física y política de Chile.* 28 vols. Paris: privately published, 1844–1871. A favorable account of O'Higgins.

HUMPHREYS, R. A. *Liberation In South America, 1806–1827. The Career of James Paroissien.* London: The University of London, 1952. Physician Paroissien was present at several important military events in O'Higgins' life.

MEHEGAN, JOHN J. *O'Higgins of Chile.* London: J. & J. Bennett, Ltd., 1913. A sound but superficial study of O'Higgins.

MITRE, BARTOLOMÉ. *Historia de San Martín y de la emancipación Sud-Americana.* Many editions. The classic study of San Martín. Mitre credits O'Higgins when he deserves it, but points out his mistakes.

MONTANER BELLO, RICARDO. *Historia diplomática de la independencia de Chile.* Santiago: Editorial Andrés Bello, 1961. The best single-volume study of the subject.

ORREGO VICUÑA, EUGENIO. *El espiritu constitucional de la administración O'Higgins.* Santiago: Imprenta Cervantes, 1924. This is an excellent and impressively scholarly study. As in the following work, the author is enthused with O'Higgins and finds much to admire in him.

————. *O'Higgins. Vida y Tiempo.* Buenos Aires: Editorial Losada, S. A., 1946. It compares favorably with Eyzaguirre's biography.

SEGALL, MARCELO R. "Las luchas de las clases en las primeras décadas de la República, 1810–1846," in *Anales de la Universidad de Chile,* No. 125 (Primer Trimestre de 1962), 175–218. An evocative study written with a Marxist orientation.

VICUÑA MACKENNA, BENJAMÍN. *El ostracismo del general d. Bernardo O'Higgins.* n.p., 1860. An excellent account by one of Chile's most famous and important nineteenth-century liberal historians. All succeeding studies owe a debt to this work. He is favorable to O'Higgins, but points out his weaknesses. The book eventually became *Vida del Capitán General de Chile don Bernardo O'Higgins.* Published in 1882, this book is much like its predecessor. See also his *La Guerra A Muerte,* Vol. XV in *Obras completas De Vicuña Mackenna.* Santiago, 1940.

Index